# CONTENTS

## Ships in Focus Publications

*Correspondence and editorial:*
Roy Fenton
18 Durrington Avenue
London SW20 8NT
020 8879 3527
record@rfenton.co.uk

*Orders and photographic:*
John & Marion Clarkson
18 Franklands, Longton
Preston PR4 5PD
01772 612855
shipsinfocus@btinternet.com

Printed by Amadeus Press Ltd.,
Cleckheaton, Yorkshire.
Designed by Hugh Smallwood, John Clarkson
and Roy Fenton.

SHIPS IN FOCUS RECORD
**ISBN** 978-0-9928263-3-8

## SUBSCRIPTION RATES FOR RECORD

Readers can start their subscription with any
issue, and are welcome to backdate it to receive
previous issues.

|  | 3 issues | 4 issues |
|---|---|---|
| UK | £27 | £35 |
| Europe (airmail) | £29 | £38 |
| Rest of the world (surface mail) | £29 | £38 |
| Rest of the world (airmail) | £35 | £46 |

# SHIPS IN FOCUS

### March 2015

True or false: the more recent an event, the easi[...]
It might be thought, for instance, that researchin[...] [...]ory of a ship, a
company or a shipping service is easier if it was in the very recent past. This
is certainly true in the case of the article on the last years of Bank Line in this
issue, when author Malcolm Cranfield could call on the help of colleagues
and friends in the shipping industry to do a masterful job of unravelling the
complexity of ships chartered in, chartered out, and joint services that came
and went over a relatively short period.

However, experience with our recently-published Blue Star
book was less positive. Here we were often dealing with complex financial
transactions, involving an organisation which, to put it politely, has never
welcomed its affairs being examined in detail. For this reason, although
it included a history of the company, the book's focus was on the ships
themselves, as reflected in the title 'Blue Star Line – A Fleet History'.

But even when tracing the histories of the more recent ships
themselves, there were contradictions and uncertainties. Part of this arose
because of the complexity of the modern shipping industry. Contemporary
sources of information now routinely quote seven categories of owner,
operator or manager for each ship, and quite where the boundaries lie
between these bodies is by no means apparent. The registered owner often
seems to be very distantly, if at all, related to the operator, with third-party
managers even more remote, and seemingly changing frequently as ships
move between trades. To confound matters further, information sources
available may well quote quite different managers and operators for the same
ship at the same time. In contrast, researching a ship from a period up to
about 50 years ago is much more straightforward: even if owned by a single-
ship company the details of its managers were almost always available and
reliable, and management continued year after year. With today's ships – and
the reefers listed in the latter part of Blue Star Line were a case in point –
the researcher has to use skill and judgement in tracing a history, and has
to accept that the interpretation of the information by others might well be
different.

In this issue we continue the theme which began with the article
on Coronel and the Falklands in 'Record' 59, and reflect further on the impact
of the First World War on shipping in the feature on the Instones, whose
fortune was made from ships during the conflict, notwithstanding two rather
disastrous ventures. And with our recent log-jam of articles over, we resume
our leisurely photographic perambulation around the ports of Devon and
Cornwall in South West Scenes, which looks at Par and Charlestown. Our
notional 'volume' ends with this issue, and we include the customary index,
with eight extra pages to accommodate it plus some self-indulgence from the
editors. May we also remind potential contributors that, with a new volume
of 'Record' beginning with number 61, there is still plenty of space yet to fill!
John Clarkson                                                              Roy Fenton

*Autocarrier* sailing from Calais (page 200). *[J. and M.Clarkson collection]*

# SOUTH WEST SCENES
## 5. Par and Charlestown

Until recently, the small harbour of Par was busy with coasters loading china clay. A victim of globalisation - or as it is less politely known, corporate greed - Par closed in 2007 after its main user, English China Clays, was sold to French owners who sourced much of their raw materials from South America.

Building Par harbour began in the 1830s, when the entrepreneur Thomas Treffry determined to build an outlet for granite and copper ore from local quarries and mines. He succeeded despite those who told him his port would be vulnerable to winds from the south east. These winds helped seal the fate of nearby Pentewan, causing sand to pile up in its narrow entrance channel. Treffry also built a canal, and later a railway, from his mines to Par harbour.

Whereas many Cornish harbours fell on hard times as granite and ore exports declined, Par benefitted from the growth in china clay shipments, which had begun within two decades of its construction. This trade dominated the port until closure, indeed the only other commodities

handled were oil, brought coastwise, and the occasional cargo of timber. There were eventually seven berths, reduced from the 13 the port could once accommodate as ships became larger and larger: Par could take ships up to 300 feet in length.

English China Clays came to own the tidal port, along with Fowey, and used Par for smaller shipments to European ports, whilst Fowey took bigger vessels for longer voyages. Clay was brought to Par from the workings either in dry bulk form, or as a slurry through a pipeline.

In the scene above, with the original number of berths in operation, more than a dozen ketches and schooners are in port, with what appears to be a paddle tug alongside one of the sailing vessels against the quay in the background. One of the few names that can be read with certainty is that of the Glasgow-registered *Mary* in the foreground. This was the commonest name for a British ship in the nineteenth century, and the 1890 'Mercantile Navy List' records 153, three of them registered in Glasgow. However, one of these is owned in Cornwall, a schooner

built at Ardrossan in 1877 and registered to a Samuel Yeo of Tywardreath. In 1919 she was sold to Belgium becoming *Odette*, but within a year returned to Devon ownership as the *Cobden* of Plymouth. Martin Benn's very useful 'Closing Down Sail' records that her final owner came from Guernsey, to where she was outward bound from Hull with coal when she was sank in the Humber on 16th January 1923 after colliding with a locally owned steam trawler.

The ketch to the far right is the Bristol-registered *J. Milton*, built at Saul on the River Severn in 1872, and owned in 1890 by one of the Nurse family of Bridgwater. James Nurse's delightful book 'The Nurse Family of Bridgwater and their Ships' lists her as being owned by the Nurses from 1889 to 1930, after which she was fitted with an auxiliary oil engine and renamed *Borderstar*. Her hull lasted until 1958, latterly as a fender barge in Barry Docks, and was only broken up after it was crushed and sunk by another ship.

Photographs are from the editors' collections, unless otherwise credited.

Par is not quite as busy here, but a total of ten motor coasters can be picked out. Nearest the camera is the Dublin-registered *Joan T*, owned by Michael J. Tyrrell of Arklow from 1973 to 1985. Built in the Netherlands in 1959, she had previously been named *Scheldt* and *Thomas M*. Under the name *Elfi* she is recorded as foundering in March 1987. To her right is *Vauban*, a coaster with impeccable Cornish connections as she had been built in 1962 by Brazen Island Shipyard Ltd. near Fowey. *Vauban* (below), still with mainmast had a number of owners, but it is most likely that when photographed she was with Cornish Shipping Ltd. of Plymouth, who had her from 1971 to 1980. As *Rolston* she was broken up on the Humber in 1987.

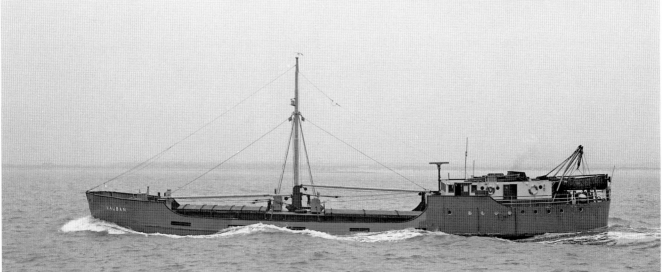

A view from the opposite direction includes seven coasters, of which (from right to left) *Vliestroom* (500/1957), *Fylrix* (598/1962) and *Anna Sietas* (471/1952) can be identified with confidence. *Vliestroom* belonged to N.V. Hollandsche Stoomboot Maatschappij of Amsterdam, a company whose coasters were once familiar as operating regular liner services to British ports, but which did not disdain a return cargo of china clay. The Arnhem-built shelter decker was converted to a cattle carrier in 1969, and as *Frisian Express* lasted until broken up at Vigo in 1989. Rix's *Fylrix* was unfortunate enough to founder on 22nd November 1984 in Plymouth Sound. *Anna Sietas* was built at Neuenfelde, lengthened in 1955 and sold in 1971, becoming *Ketty*, *Julia S*, and finally *Southern Cross*, being deleted from register books in 1994.

Par harbour is again well occupied. Beginning at the left, the first coaster is an Empire F type owned by Everard. Next is the British motor coaster *Farndale* (207/1933). She was built by J. Koster at Groningen, and bought on the stocks by Tyne-Tees Steam Shipping Co. Ltd. and carried the name *Etal* until 1946. As *Farndale* she was registered in the ownership of Mrs M.C. Sinnott, becoming part of a small fleet managed in Cardiff by the Tyrrell family. Around 1958 she was sold, the new owner retaining her name but putting her under the currently fashionable flag-of-convenience of Costa Rica.

Beyond *Farndale* are two Everard motor coasters.

The Groningen-registered coaster on the quay to the right is *Rubato* (498/1955). She was completed at Martenshoek for W. Schuitema and D. Schothorst with management by N.V. 'Carebeka', an arrangement which survived until 1970. After a succession of further names under Dutch or Greek ownership, she was sold for scrap in 1969. The building year of *Rubato* and the sale date of *Farndale* date this photograph to between 1955 and 1958.
Note on the quay to the right of *Rubato* the steam crane and the diminutive tank locomotive, one of two Bagnall 0-4-0 saddle tanks, *Alfred* and *Judy,* built for the port.

One of Par's best known ships was the Padstow-built schooner *Katie* of 1881, seen in 1933. She sailed from Par in August 1948 for Copenhagen, where she languished for many years. Discovered in 1972, a group of enthusasts aimed to bring her back to Cornwall for restoration, but unfortunately she foundered en route whilst under tow.

The tiny harbour of Charlestown was constructed to plans of John Smeaton between 1791 and 1799 to serve local copper mines. Like nearby Par, it also prospered through the china clay trade, but was seriously restricted by its diminutive size, and lack of a rail connection.

In the late 1930s, the steamers *Croham* (391/1912) and *Broom* (347/1934) sit beyond the lock gates whilst a Dutch motor coaster can be seen at the far end of the dock (top). *Croham* was built at Paisley as *Risedale* and, despite her registration, she was owned in Newcastle by John Cole when photographed. Three further names later, she was broken up at Sunderland in 1952. *Broom* spent her entire life with Joseph Fisher and Sons Ltd. of Newry and was demolished at Barrow-in-Furness in late 1954.

44499. ST. AUSTELL: CHARLESTOWN HARBOUR, SHIPPING CHINA CLAY.

The cart has brought down china clay in bags which are being split open before the clay is slid down the chute into the hold of a steam coaster (middle). Sliding the bags down the chute would have invited disaster: they would simply have burst, leaving an even worse white mess than is already on the quay in this photograph.

Here, one of Everard's motor coasters of the 1930s enters the harbour (bottom). Judging by the numbers on the breakwater, watching ships negotiating the harbour entrance and making the acute turn into the dock was a popular spectator sport.

A view into the harbour reveals four sailing vessels or auxiliaries almost filling Charlestown (top). The only one which can be identified is the Terneuzen-registered *Zeehond*, whose stern helpfully identifies her home port as being in Holland. A steel auxiliary schooner of 188 gt whose name and port of registration fits is listed in the 1924 'Lloyd's Register'. She was built in 1914 as a pure sailing vessel by J.J. Pattje & Zoon at Waterhuizen. By 1926 she has been sold and re-registered at Groningen.

Everard's *Alf Everard* was built at Yarmouth in 1925 as a steel spritsail barge, only to be converted into a small motor coaster in 1943 (middle). She was sunk in collision with Ellerman's *City of Johannesburg* (8,207/1947) on Christmas Eve, 1953.

The Dutch coaster *Meta* (298/1934) in Charlestown during June 1970 (bottom). She had been built at Delfzijl as *Grunda* and carried the name *Amigo* from 1940 until 1963. As *Meta* she was lengthened in 1964, somewhat marring her classic hull shape. She was broken up in 1972. Note how crude were loading facilities at Charlestown. The china clay was simply tipped from vehicles standing on a public road down a chute into the hold of a waiting vessel.

A relatively modern Everard motor coaster is seen in Charlestown on 1st August 1970, the *Fixity* (199/1966), one of a group built by Fellows and Co. Ltd. of Great Yarmouth. In 1976 *Fixity* was sold to a company building oil rigs and given the somewhat more romantic name of *Kirstie of Kishorn*. Despite her size, she later crossed the North Atlantic to work around Newfoundland as *Bacalac Transport*. She was last heard of in 1994 under the Panama flag as *Viveros II*. [Peter L. White]

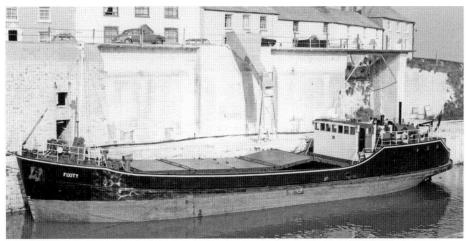

*Lady Sheena* (200/1966) was built at Bergum in the Netherlands for Thomas Watson (Shipping) Ltd. Sold in 1976 by this long-established Rochester owner (the company originally operated sailing barges), *Lady Sheena* had a bewildering variety of further names, mostly under the British flag. She was last heard of as *Raider*, but no owner has been listed since 1990.

The photograph is dated June 1972, and shows that an extra clay chute has been installed.

Charlestown's ability to take only the smallest coasters saw its trade decline and fail as fewer and fewer little ships were built, and those in existence became increasingly uneconomic. The port loaded its last cargo of china clay in 2000, but has since become a base for sailing vessels and has been used as a film set. One of the last coasters to load is at the far end of the dock, aft of which are two small sailing vessels, at least one appearing to be a replica. This view emphases the tortuous nature of the entrance to Charlestown: getting the coaster in must have been a very tight fit.

On 1st May 1929 the Southern Railway introduced a new service for cross-Channel cars, using *Whitstable* from Folkestone and a chartered vessel from Dover, and the following June the company invited tenders for a new cargo vessel intended to be a replacement for the aged *Walmer*. By October the design had been changed to that of a cargo steamer with passenger accommodation, for the construction of which D. and W. Henderson secured the contract and laid the keel of what was originally to be called *Camberley* but which was launched in February 1931 as *Autocarrier*. As if to underline her status as a cargo vessel, she first reached Dover in March laden with coal which was discharged at the Admiralty Pier extension. She had the ability to stow up to 35 crane-loaded cars and was the first cross-Channel vessel specifically designed for the carriage of vehicles and their passengers. After an inaugural crossing the previous day,

*Autocarrier* entered scheduled service on the last day of March and thereafter made a single 1¾-hour crossing in each direction, departing Dover at 12:15 and Calais at 16:00. The passenger fare was 10 shillings (50p), with a charge of less than £2.00 being made for transporting a car not exceeding 8 feet 6 inches in length. She offered, for up to 120 passengers, accommodation in a general saloon and bar and, on the deck below, two saloons, one for gentlemen and the other for ladies, both fitted with sofa seating. At that time these features were praised by the press as providing the last word in cross-Channel travel for motorists, although in due course even her owners conceded that her facilities had become distinctly inadequate. Her overall length was the same as that of the 1920s cargo ships, some of which could carry a maximum of 28 cars and up to 12 passengers.

Early in 1930 *Cherbourg* left the fleet and a decline in cargo tonnage

from just over 12,000 in 1931 to less than 3,600 in 1932 resulted in serious losses on the Southampton to Honfleur service and its discontinuation that September. The following month it was decided that, as a result of the cost of implementing new safety regulations and because of import restrictions from France following a Colorado beetle outbreak, *Ada* and *Bertha* should also be disposed of but it took more than 12 months for this to be achieved. In April 1933 the name *Brittany* was required for a new Southern Railway passenger ship but, bearing the new name *Aldershot*, the former *Brittany* continued her cargo sailings until the introduction of a Dover-Dunkirk train ferry service freed *Minster* for transfer to Southampton towards the end of 1936. The sale of *Aldershot* brought to an end a railway career which had started by her grounding outside Newhaven on her delivery voyage from Hull in 1910. Her disposal, following that of *Walmer* the previous year, reduced the average age of the cargo fleet to 11, which was a very significant improvement on the 26 years of the vessels which the company had inherited. The four remaining Southampton cargo ships completed 679 single crossings in 1937, sailed over 78,600 nautical miles and carried almost 100,000 tons of cargo, over 80% of it to or from the Channel Islands. As was customary to cope with seasonal demand on the Southampton routes, the Southern Railway chartered in tonnage which that year handled 7,900 tons of cargo. Cross-Channel holiday traffic was sufficiently brisk in July 1938 to justify the Friday evening departure of no fewer than seven passenger ships from Southampton and these were supplemented by *Fratton* carrying passengers' cars to Le Havre and *Haslemere* performing the same function to St Malo.

**Second World War service**
After the outbreak of the Second World War in September 1939, *Autocarrier* and five other cargo vessels continued serving France from Folkestone until *Deal*, *Maidstone* and *Tonbridge* were

The first Channel steamer designed to carry cars and their passengers, *Autocarrier* is shown here sharing a Southampton dry dock with *Brittany*, the 1933 passenger ship which caused the cargo ship of that name to become *Aldershot*. [*Author's collection*]

moved westwards for the late May 1940 opening of a new cargo service. This was on the 138-mile route between Plymouth and St Malo, using at the former port two steam cranes which had been dismantled and transported from Folkestone. The railways had provided a commercial service across the western Channel practically without a break during the First World War and the Southern Railway had hopes of repeating this, if necessary replacing St Malo by a port on the French Atlantic coast. The three cargo ships remaining in the Strait of Dover were conveniently placed to assist with the massive military evacuation from north east France. *Hythe* crossed to Dunkirk harbour on 31st May and returned to Dover packed with British, French and Belgian soldiers, in marked contrast to *Whitstable* which, despite waiting over six hours close inshore off a beach being subjected to severe bombardment that same day, found only 14 troops to rescue. The timing of *Autocarrier*'s second round trip to Dunkirk made her one of the last vessels to reach Dover as the evacuation ended on 4th June, when she disembarked 712 servicemen. These three ships then moved westwards amid an increasingly deteriorating military situation, which forced *Autocarrier* to close the scheduled service from St Malo to Jersey on 14th June and, two days later, for *Deal* and *Maidstone* each to embark 450 British troops and leave the Breton port for Plymouth. In case of a need for small ships to facilitate a beach evacuation of British servicemen still in western France, *Hythe* and *Whitstable* were ordered to the Bay of Biscay but their services were not required because the large ports were temporarily still functioning. On the 20th and 21st June all the cargo ships, except *Hythe*, were allocated to evacuate civilians who wished to leave the Channel Islands, with the 250 Guernsey women and children aboard *Tonbridge* being subjected to a 30-hour delay before being allowed to enter Weymouth harbour. During a very temporary resumption of shipping normality, *Ringwood* had loaded a full cargo of produce when Guernsey harbour was attacked by aircraft on 28th June as a prelude to German occupation of the Channel Isles. Carrying numerous bullet scars, *Ringwood* escaped to Southampton and the railway steamer link was severed for almost five years.

After sailing across the Strait of Dover for 12 years, *Minster* was transferred to the Southampton routes in 1936 and became a war loss off the Normandy beaches in June 1944. *[National Maritime Museum P20917]*

On her final Guernsey call in June 1940 *Ringwood* was attacked by German aircraft: that event was in sharp contrast to her serene post-war departure pictured here. *[Author's collection]*

Seen in 1942 as a Royal Navy Balloon Barrage Ship, *Fratton* was commended for escorting 15 consecutive convoys between the Thames and the Solent without a single serious defect. *[Imperial War Museum HU1335]*

In August 1940 *Fratton* was commissioned to join the Channel Mobile Balloon Barrage service, designed to protect from low level air attack coastal convoys sailing between the Solent and the Thames Estuary and it was noted that she escorted 15 consecutive convoys without a single serious defect. In November she was joined by *Haslemere*, which came under fire that month when a shell from a German long-range gun on the French coast burst close to her port bow, wounding two officers, one fatally, and causing splinter damage to her hull, funnel and superstructure. This had been one of at least 170 shells aimed at the convoy during a four-hour period. *Deal* was added to this fleet in May 1941 and had the satisfaction of at least seriously damaging one enemy aircraft with her three anti-aircraft guns but had the later misfortune of colliding with a naval trawler which sank off Dover. During air raids on Plymouth in 1941, where both vessels were laid up, *Whitstable*'s deckhouse was destroyed, while *Maidstone* sustained engine room damage from one bomb explosion and external damage from another. *Maidstone* was commissioned as HMS *Bungay* that September and served with the Balloon Barrage fleet until its withdrawal in May 1943, whereupon *Fratton* and *Haslemere* became commodore's ships with coastal convoys, while *Deal* and *Maidstone* were paid off. *Haslemere*'s

appearance in 1942 was altered with disruptive camouflage paint; a short mast between her bridge and funnel; six life rafts and light anti-aircraft guns in bandstands, one at her bow and two in raised positions immediately forward of her after hold. Three days after *Haslemere* had been commissioned in November 1940, *Minster* followed suit for service as a net layer and, at Gosport in January 1941, sustained bomb blast damage to her deckhouses. Her duties subsequently involved three years of net laying and allied assignments in coastal waters between Dover and Scapa Flow; as well as off Iceland, the Faeroe Islands and the Scottish west coast. *Tonbridge*, commissioned for similar duties in November 1940, had just completed laying a net defence obstruction off Sheringham when a German aircraft hit her with two bombs on 22nd August 1941 and she sank with the loss of 32 lives. As a replacement, *Ringwood*, which had been employed transporting military stores across the Irish Sea from May 1941, was commissioned in February 1942 to undertake similar work to that described above for *Minster*. From July 1941 *Autocarrier* was based at the fleet anchorage at Scapa Flow and became a popular ship providing recreational facilities for the crews of fleet auxiliaries.

Four Southern Railway cargo ships reached the Normandy coast within 24 hours of the D-Day landings in June 1944. *Fratton* and *Haslemere*

formed part of the fleet in charge of the Mulberry Harbours, which were towed across the English Channel, with *Minster* and *Ringwood* being responsible for the placement of moorings and buoys until 8th June, when the former was lost as a result of a mine explosion. *Fratton* became the victim of a torpedo attack and went down stern-first on 18th August 1944. *Haslemere* and *Ringwood* survived their time off the Normandy beaches and, whereas the former was paid off, in 1945 *Ringwood* was assigned to operations which involved the laying of miles of wire attached to floats to the west of Orkney and Shetland, with the object of slicing off the schnorkel masts of U-boats. Meanwhile, *Whitstable* had visited Seine Bay under assignment to carry United States Navy salvage gear and personnel and, after completing this in October 1944, was for a short time replaced by *Maidstone*. When not required for naval deployment the cargo fleet was either laid up or allocated cargo-carrying duties. *Whitstable*, for instance, had acted as relief vessel on the Penzance-Isles of Scilly route in late 1941, then sailed between Fishguard and Rosslare in 1942 and carried milk from Larne to Cairnryan early in 1945. Carrying government cargo, *Hythe* had performed sailings to Belfast and Londonderry from Preston and was later transferred to the Leith-Orkney route, on which she encountered such heavy seas in a November 1943 crossing that her starboard lifeboat was washed overboard.

### Services re-established

As soon as possible after the end of the war in Europe in May 1945 the Southern Railway set about re-establishing its English Channel cargo services. *Haslemere* was the first ship to become available and, with her hull still painted wartime grey, left Southampton for the Channel Islands on 22nd June. *Deal* followed her three days later and *Whitstable* on 17th July. When *Hythe* and *Maidstone* were released, the company restored a cargo and mail service between Folkestone and Calais on 9th August that year but it was not until 4th March 1946 that *Hythe* could reopen cargo sailings to Boulogne, by which time *Deal* was once again Folkestone-based. In November 1945 the fore part of *Haslemere* was severely damaged when she struck a rock in the Channel Islands, an accident which put her out

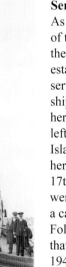

On war service, *Autocarrier* was a Welfare Ship at the fleet anchorage in Scapa Flow. Here she is alongside one vessel in 1943, with the crew of another about to depart by tender. *[Imperial War Museum A17401]*

of service for more than four months. *Autocarrier* started her first post-war cargo sailing from Southampton to Jersey on 10th December 1945 and this round trip was quickly followed by the first of six special crossings to the Channel Island of Alderney, spread over the subsequent seven months. Meanwhile, on 27th November 1945, *Whitstable* had carried out the first post-war Jersey-France sailing, carrying six passengers to Granville, the only port available until sufficient war damage repairs could be completed to enable St Malo to be opened on 16th April 1946. *Autocarrier* served the Jersey-France route on a fortnightly frequency between January and May 1946 before, on 1st August, providing a special service for motorists to the continent from Folkestone, for which her car capacity was limited to 24 because of the need to allocate additional crew space. She continued this employment until the end of October and restarted again in April 1947 having, during part of the intervening January and February, been assigned to restore post-war sailings to Le Havre from Southampton. The late release from naval service of *Ringwood* delayed her return to Channel Islands service until June 1946 and made her the last cargo steamer to resume peacetime sailings. On 6th June 1947 *Whitstable* started a Dover-Calais cargo service, before, in October, switching her French destination to Dunkirk, sailing on alternate days until the train ferry service could be resumed: soon thereafter Southampton became her main base.

The wartime loss of three cargo vessels more than justified the July 1945 order of a new ship designed

The first railway cargo ship to resume service to the Channel Islands in June 1945, *Haslemere* leaves Southampton with her hull painted a wartime grey but her funnel restored to peacetime buff with black top. *[Author's collection]*

primarily for the Southampton-Channel Islands service but suitable for use on any English Channel route, as would be demonstrated from time to time during her career. The building cost increased by more than £32,000 during the 29 months before delivery could be made and the new vessel, named *Winchester*, commenced her first sailing to Jersey on 1st December 1947, exactly one month before railway nationalisation. Finally costing £215,154, *Winchester* was a 1,149 gross ton motor vessel with a cargo space of 49,450 cubic feet, details which made an interesting contrast with the £12,855 cost of the 388-ton *Cherbourg* of 1873, which had 21,080 cubic feet cargo capacity. To cater for car traffic across the Strait of Dover, *Autocarrier* was displaced by a larger capacity passenger ship but use of her car-carrying capability was found from Southampton to both Le Havre and St Malo in summer 1949 and, on the latter route, with twice-weekly crossings the following year. She was to have inaugurated car ferry sailings between Holyhead and Ireland in 1954 but she became surplus to requirements after this plan had been dropped. Also no longer required on the English Channel, *Maidstone* was moved to Irish waters in 1953 to sail from Heysham and, in the autumns of 1954 and 1955, *Hythe* was assigned as relief vessel on the Harwich-Antwerp-Rotterdam route. She did not meet traffic requirements there and her limited space for containers resulted in her withdrawal from English Channel service and disposal early in 1956. Her place that year on Harwich relief duty was taken firstly by *Maidstone*, then by *Ringwood*, the latter vessel being capable of handling livestock traffic. In July 1958 *Maidstone* was surplus to requirements; *Whitstable* was made available for sale the following March, with *Haslemere* and *Ringwood* following suit later that same year. *Deal*'s service from Folkestone, initially due to end in June 1959, was

The first new cargo vessel for 19 years and the first to be diesel-driven, the 1947 *Winchester* was an addition to the fleet immediately prior to railway nationalisation. *[Author's collection]*

in fact extended until 1963, making her the last survivor of her class of nine 1920s sisters, each of which, excluding war losses, had on average served the railways more than 33 years. The only former Southern Railway vessel then remaining in the railway fleet was the 1947-built *Winchester*. Her sale in 1971 launched her into a most surprising new career sailing Greek waters in Chandris colours as the passenger excursion vessel *Radiosa*, with the result that it was not until 1988 that the last ship to join the Southern Railway fleet finally met her end.

## Fleet list part 2: vessels built for the Southern Railway Company, 1924-1947

*On 1st January 1948 surviving vessels began operating for the British Transport Commission. The act nationalising the Southern Railway ships was dated 6th August 1947 but, as with the 1923 grouping, registration of the ships under the new ownership was delayed for most of the vessels until 21st July 1948.*

### AUTOCARRIER 1931-1954
O.N. 162557 822g 329n.
220·3 x 35.6 x 14.1 feet.
Cargo capacity: 47,410 cubic feet.
Two T. 3-cyl. by D. and W. Henderson and Co. Ltd., Glasgow; 279 NHP, 2,000 IHP, 15 knots.

*5.2.1931:* Launched by D. and W. Henderson and Co. Ltd., Glasgow (Yard No. 912).
*13.3.1931:* Registered in the ownership of the Southern Railway Company, London as AUTOCARRIER for Strait of Dover services. She cost £49,976.
*26.3.1931:* Arrived Dover.
*30.3.1931:* Inaugural Dover to Calais crossing, prior to the start of scheduled sailings the following day.
*16-17.9.1935:* Collided with Calais pier head in severe gale during the night.
*14.2.1936:* Collided with company's TONBRIDGE outside Calais whilst carrying Indian mails.
*28.2.1938:* In collision with tanker INVERITCHEN (708/1920) in Southampton Water whilst on passage from Dover to Southampton for her annual survey.
*19.5.1940:* Taken up for military service.
*20.5-3.6.1940:* Completed three round trips to Calais and one to Dunkirk.
*4.6.1940:* Arrived Dover with 712 troops after a second round trip to Dunkirk and released.
*14.6.1940:* Closed the St Malo to Jersey scheduled service.
*20.6.1940:* Left Jersey for Southampton with evacuees, then resumed commercial sailings.
*28.6.1940:* Arrived Southampton from Jersey with potatoes and laid up.
*19.5.1941:* Taken up for government service.
*17.7.1941:* Arrived Scapa Flow to serve as a welfare ship for officers and men of non-commissioned fleet auxiliaries.
*6.12.1945:* Released after refit at Victoria Dock, London.
*10.12.1945:* Left Southampton for Jersey to resume peacetime service.
*14.12.1945-15.7.1946:* Undertook cargo and

passenger sailings including Southampton-Alderney and Jersey-France.
*1.8.1946:* Inaugurated post-war car ferry service between Folkestone and Boulogne, with sailings continuing until 31.10.1946.
*19.12.1946-1.3.1947:* Sailed fortnightly on Jersey to St. Malo route.
*7.1.1947:* Inaugurated post-war sailings between Southampton and Le Havre, initially for cargo then fortnightly for passengers until 26.2.1947.
*1.4-31.10.1947:* Folkestone-Boulogne car ferry service.
*1.1.1948:* Transferred to the British Transport Commission, London.
*1954:* Sold for breaking up in Belgium.
*29.7.1954:* Register closed on sale for breaking up.
*7.8.1954:* Arrived at Ghent to be broken up by Van Heyghen Frères.

### DEAL (2) 1928-1963
O.N. 160387 688g 270n.
220.5 x 33.7 x 14.2 feet.
Cargo capacity: 30,043 cubic feet.
Two x T. 3-cyl. by D. and W. Henderson and Co. Ltd., Glasgow; 281 NHP, 1,850 IHP, 15 knots.

*10.2.1928:* Launched by D. and W. Henderson and Co. Ltd., Glasgow (Yard No. 818).
*12.3.1928:* Registered in the ownership of the Southern Railway Company, London as DEAL for Strait of Dover services.
*21.3.1928:* Stranded for four hours on rocks near Portavogie, County Down during delivery voyage.
*27.4.1928:* After damage repaired by builders, delivered at Southampton at a cost of £41,810.
*1929-1939:* On Strait of Dover service without incident.

In August 1946, *Autocarrier* re-established a car ferry connection across the Strait of Dover and the following winter was used to reopen the passenger and cargo service to Le Havre from Southampton. *[Author's collection]*

The last of nine similar ships to join the fleet, *Deal* became the sole survivor of her class during the three years leading up to her withdrawal in 1963. *[Fotoflite incorporating Skyfotos]*

*23.5.1940:* Left Folkestone for Southampton.

*30.5.1940:* Left Southampton for St Malo to operate a new cargo service to Plymouth.

*16.6.1940:* Left St Malo for Plymouth with 450 British troops.

*21.6.1940:* Left Guernsey for Weymouth with civilian evacuees.

*27.6.1940:* Arrived Plymouth from Jersey and laid up. Subsequently damaged by bombs at Plymouth.

*16.5.1941:* Taken up for naval service as a balloon barrage ship.

*22.5.1941:* Two miles west of the Needles, opened fire on a German aircraft which was seen to be in flames before disappearing.

*7.7.1941:* Commissioned at Southampton as HMS DEAL.

*16.6.1942:* Damaged in collision with the minesweeping trawler TRANQUIL which sank whilst towing barges off Dover.

*21.5.1943:* Released from requisition and laid up.

*28.11.43:* Left Southampton for Irish Sea service.

*5.12.1943:* Undertook various sailings including Fishguard to Cork and Manchester to Belfast.

*6.2.1944:* Samson post damaged when port side hit by the steamer EMPIRE NIGEL (7,067/1920) at Eastham.

*22.4.1944:* Began sailing between Heysham and Belfast.

*23.6.1945:* Released from requisition after refit at Liverpool.

*25.6.1945:* Left Southampton for the Channel Islands on resumption of Southern Railway service.

*11.1945:* Returned to Strait of Dover services.

*1.1.1948:* Transferred to the British Transport Commission, London.

*21.5.1963:* Register closed on sale for breaking up.

*22.5.1963:* Arrived at Ghent to be broken up by Van Heyghen Frères.

**FRATTON 1925-1944**

O.N. 147039  757g 305n.

220·3 x 33.6 x 14.2 feet.

Cargo capacity 33,360 cubic feet.

Two T.3-cyl. by D. and W. Henderson and Co. Ltd., Glasgow; 281 NHP, 1,850 IHP, 15 knots.

*18.8.1925:* Launched by D. and W. Henderson and Co. Ltd., Glasgow (Yard No. 720).

*24.9.1925:* Registered in the ownership of the Southern Railway, London as FRATTON.

*27.9.1925:* Delivered for Southampton services at a cost of £42,250

*7.10.1927:* Bottom plates damaged by striking a rock on the approaches to St Malo whilst crossing from Southampton.

*1928-1939:* On Southampton service without serious incident.

*21.6.1940:* Left Guernsey for Weymouth with civilian evacuees.

*28.6.1940:* Left Southampton until German bombing of the Channel Islands caused her to be turned back.

*8.1940:* Taken up for naval service as a Balloon Barrage Ship.

*12.8.1940:* Commissioned at Southampton as HMS FRATTON.

*6.2.1942:* In collision with the steamer RUDMORE (969/1911) in the Thames Estuary.

*20.5.1943:* Became commodore's ship for coastal convoys.

*4.1944:* Accommodation ship.

*7.6.1944:* Arrived off the Normandy coast as a Mulberry Harbour Bombardon Control Ship.

*18.8.1944:* Sank stern first in four minutes after being hit port side aft by a German piloted 'Neger' torpedo whilst at anchor off Arromanches.

*22.3.1945:* Register closed.

*Fratton. [World Ship Society Ltd.]*

205

## HASLEMERE 1925-1959

O.N. 148636 756g 305n.
220.3 x 33.7 x 16.2 feet.
Cargo capacity 33,360 cubic feet.
Two T.3-cyl. by D. and W. Henderson and Co. Ltd., Glasgow; 281 NHP, 1,850 IHP, 15 knots.
*22.5.1925:* Launched by D. and W. Henderson and Co. Ltd., Meadowside, Glasgow (Yard No. 719M).
*1.7.1925:* Registered in the ownership of the Southern Railway Company, London as DEAL.
*5.7.1925:* Delivered at Southampton at a cost of £42,250 for Southampton services.
*9.11.1925:* Port bow sustained damage against the lock entrance when entering Le Havre in boisterous weather.
*15.4.1926:* Briefly touched ground at Hurst Point on passage from Guernsey to Southampton.
*7.9.1927:* Collided in Southampton Water with the steam yacht STAR OF INDIA whilst sailing for St Malo.
*16.12.1929:* In collision with the French tug ABEILLE 6 after leaving Honfleur for Southampton.
*9.11.1931:* Put back to St Malo with rudder and starboard propeller damage in a heavy squall, after which ship reached Southampton six days later with a tug escort:
*20.6.1940:* Left Guernsey for Weymouth with civilian evacuees.
*28.6.1940:* Arrived Southampton from Guernsey and laid up.
*26.10.1940:* Taken up for naval service as a Balloon Barrage Ship.
*8.11.1940:* Commissioned at Southampton as HMS HASLEMERE.
*25.11.1940:* One officer killed and another wounded by a long-range shell burst under ship's port bow, causing damage to her hull and superstructure.
*20.5.1943:* Became commodore's ship for coastal convoys.

*7.6.1944:* Arrived off the Normandy coast as a Mulberry Harbour Bombardon Phoenix and Whale Control Ship.
*10.1944:* Laid up.
*27.3.1945:* Paid off on the Clyde.
*6.6.1945:* Released following refit by D. and W. Henderson and Co. Ltd., Glasgow.
*22.6.1945:* Left Southampton for Jersey to reopen Southern Railway Channel Islands service.
*23.11.1945:* Severely damaged fore part when hitting a rock off the island of Brecqhou whilst on passage to Southampton in poor visibility.
*12.4.1946:* Returned to service after repairs at South Shields.
*11.11.1947:* Forced to shelter for 20 hours off Lymington, Isle of Wight, owing to severe storm when outward bound.
*1.1.1948:* Transferred to the British Transport Commission, London (sale not registered until 15.7.1948).
*1959:* Sold to Vereenigde Utrechtsche Ijzerhandel for demolition.
*29.8.1959:* Arrived Rotterdam.
*5.9.1959:* Register closed.

## HYTHE 1925-1956

O.N. 148613 685g 269n.
220.6 x 33.7 x 14.2 feet.
Cargo capacity 30,043 cubic feet.
Two T.3-cyl. by D. and W. Henderson and Co. Ltd., Glasgow; 281 NHP, 1,850 IHP, 15 knots.
*24.4.1925:* Launched by D. and W. Henderson and Co. Ltd., Meadowside, Glasgow (Yard No. 706M).
*28.5.1925:* Registered in the ownership of the Southern Railway Company, London as HYTHE.
*4.6.1925:* Delivered at Southampton at a cost of £41,450 for Strait of Dover services.
*3.1 and 5.1.1931:* Touched ground when entering Calais.
*1932-1939:* On cargo service without serious incident.
*20.2.1940:* Damaged in collision with French trawler ADINE at Boulogne, where she underwent repairs.
*29.5.1940:* Taken up for military service.
*31.5.1940:* Rescued British, French and Belgian servicemen from Dunkirk East Pier and, despite a shell burst beneath her starboard quarter, safely reached Dover. The total carried being recorded as around 660 by the ship but as 749 by the authorities at Dover.
*5.6.1940:* Left Dover for Southampton.
*15.6.1940:* Left Southampton, via Plymouth, for St Nazaire for possible troop evacuations but not used.
*19.6.1940:* Released and resumed cargo service.
*28.6.1940:* Left Southampton for Jersey until German bombing of the Channel Islands caused her to be turned back, then laid up.
*11.3.1941:* Taken up at Southampton as a Military Store Ship.
*13.5.1941:* Started sailings between Preston, Belfast and Londonderry.

*Haslemere* post-war - note the radar - running between Jersey and Southampton. *[Dave Hocquard]*

*Haslemere* at Southampton in July 1959 - only a few weeks before her departure for breaking up. *[J. and M. Clarkson collection]*

Pictured in the later stages of her 31-year career, *Hythe* had been equipped with radar and her mainmast, removed during wartime service, had been restored. *[Fotoflite incorporating Skyfotos]*

*16.5.1941:* Hit by the steamer GERTIE (370/1902) in the River Ribble.
*1.1942:* Transferred to coasting and short sea service.
*16.11.1943:* On Leith to Orkney service, lost starboard lifeboat in heavy seas.
*7.8.1945:* Released after refit at Southampton.
*9.8.1945:* Reopened the Folkestone to Calais cargo service.
*4.3.1946:* Reopened the Folkestone to Boulogne cargo service.
*1.1.1948:* Transferred to the British Transport Commission, London (not registered until 21.7.1948).
*31.1.1956:* Arrived Dover for breaking up by Dover Industries Ltd.
*6.3.1957:* Register closed.

**MAIDSTONE 1926-1958**
O.N. 148754  688g 270n.
220.7 x 33.7 x 14.2 feet.
Cargo capacity 30,043 cubic feet.
Two T.3-cyl. by D. and W. Henderson and Co. Ltd., Glasgow; 281 NHP, 1,850 IHP, 15 knots.
*16.3.1926:* Launched by D. and W. Henderson and Co. Ltd., Meadowside, Glasgow (Yard No. 729).
*16.4.1926:* Registered in the ownership of the Southern Railway Company, London as MAIDSTONE.
*28.4.1926:* Delivered at Southampton at a cost of £40,800 for Strait of Dover services.
*17.11.1935:* Damaged stem and bow plating by striking Folkestone pier on arrival from Boulogne.
*26.5.1940:* Transferred to Plymouth to St Malo service.
*16.6.1940:* Left St Malo for Plymouth with 450 British troops.
*22.6.1940:* Left Guernsey for Weymouth with civilian evacuees.
*27.6.1940:* Arrived Plymouth from Jersey with potatoes and laid up.

*Maidstone. [Newall Dunn Collection]*

*21.4.1941:* Damaged by a bomb penetrating the engine room and another exploding on the Plymouth quayside.
*18.5.1941:* Towed to Falmouth for repairs.
*21.7.1941:* Taken up for naval service as a Balloon Barrage Ship.
*27.9.1941:* Commissioned as HMS BUNGAY.
*21.5.1943:* Released and laid up.
*1.11.1943:* Under original name, left Southampton for Manchester for Irish Sea service to Belfast and Dublin.
*11.8.1944:* Damaged at Princes's Dock, Liverpool.
*20.9.1944:* Further damaged at Ellesmere Port.
*16.11.1944:* Began service as a US Salvage Gear Depot Ship.
*28.11.1944:* Left Swansea for the Seine Estuary and Cherbourg.
*1.1.1945:* Completed US service.
*23.1.1945:* Began carrying milk from Larne to Cairnryan, then undertook sailings from the Mersey to Dublin.
*7.8.1945:* Released following refit at Southampton.

*9.8.1945:* Reopened the Folkestone to Calais cargo service.
*1.1.1948:* Transferred to the British Transport Commission, London (not registered until 21.7.1948).
*1958:* Sold for breaking up to Boomsche Scheepslooperij.
*19.12.1958:* Arrived Antwerp for demolition.

**MINSTER 1924-1944**
O.N. 147709  682g 267n.
220·4 x 33.6 14.1 feet.
Cargo capacity 30,340 cubic feet.
Two T.3-cyl. by D. and W. Henderson and Co. Ltd., Glasgow; 281 NHP, 1,850 IHP, 15 knots.
*17.6.1924:* Launched by D and W Henderson and Co. Ltd., Meadowside, Glasgow (Yard No. 634).
*12.8.1924:* Registered in the ownership of the Southern Railway Company, London as MINSTER.
*18.8.1924:* Delivered at Southampton, for Strait of Dover services. She cost £39,125.
*29.8.1924:* Temporarily withdrawn for engine repairs.

*Minster. [Newall Dunn collection]*

*4.12.1928:* Sustained considerable damage to plates and frames in collision with the French trawler ETOILE DU SUD at Calais.
*1929-1935:* On Strait of Dover service without serious incident.
*10.1936:* Transferred to Southampton services.
*21.6.1940:* Left Jersey for Weymouth with civilian evacuees.
*28.6.1940:* Left Southampton for Jersey until German bombing of the Channel Islands caused vessel to be turned back.
*30.8.1940:* Taken up at Southampton for naval service as a netlayer.
*11.11.1940:* Commissioned as HMS MINSTER.
*10.1.1941:* Deckhouses torn away by nearby bomb explosions whilst based at Gosport.
*19.4.1941:* Collided with HM Submarine SUNFISH whilst in convoy between Portsmouth and Hartlepool.
*21.4.1941 to 5.9.1941:* Laid nets in areas around Hartlepool, Flamborough Head, Lowestoft and Dover.
*4.10.1941 to 30.3.1942:* Laid nets at Scapa.
*24.6.1942 to 20.10.1943:* Worked in Icelandic and Scottish waters.
*16.2.1944:* Aground.
*6.3.1944:* Arrived at Skaale Fjord in the Faeroes.
*7.6.1944:* Arrived off the Normandy coast to lay mooring buoys.
*8.6.1944:* Mine explosion on port beam caused heavy loss of life, with MINSTER becoming submerged to the top of her deckhouse and salvage deemed impracticable.
*3.3.1945:* Register closed.

## RINGWOOD

O.N. 149629  755g 304n.
220.7 x 33.6 x 14.2 feet.
Cargo capacity 33,360 cubic feet.
Two T.3-cyl. by D. and W. Henderson and Co. Ltd., Glasgow; 281 NHP, 1,850 IHP, 15 knots.
*13.4.1926:* Launched by D. and W. Henderson and Co. Ltd., Meadowside, Glasgow (Yard No. 730).
*14.6.1926:* Delivered to the Southern Railway Company, London as RINGWOOD at a cost of £43,415 for Southampton services.
*4.8.1935:* Stood by passenger steamer PRINCESS ENA (1,198/1906) which sank whilst on passage from Jersey to St Malo.
*21.6.1940:* Left Jersey for Weymouth with civilian evacuees.
*28.6.1940:* At Guernsey after loading a full cargo of produce, one crew member, whilst ashore, injured and vessel damaged by bullets when island attacked by aircraft, as a prelude to German occupation.
*29.6.1940:* Arrived Southampton and laid up.
*11.3.1941:* Taken up as a Military Store Ship.

*25.4.1941:* Left Southampton for Irish Sea service, initially based at Preston.
*23.9.1941:* Transferred to naval service as a netlayer.
*6.2.1942:* Commissioned as HMS RINGWOOD.
*19.2.1942:* Developed engine defects.
*17.3.1942:* Began laying nets at Scapa, the Faeroes and in Scottish waters.
*22.3.1943:* Sustained bottom damage in collision with trawler ELENA.
*25.11.1943:* Based in the Portsmouth area.
*16.1.1944:* In collision with DREDGER No. 64.
*7.6.1944:* Arrived off the Normandy coast to lay mooring buoys.
*9.11.1944:* Returned to Scottish waters.
*5.1.1945:* Arrived Scapa with considerable heavy weather damage to officer's quarters aft.
*5.3.1945:* Allocated to operations west of Orkney and Shetland involving the laying of miles of wire attached to floats to slice off the schnorkel masts of U-boats.
*5.12.1945:* Paid off.
*4.6.1946:* Released after refit in London.
*10.6.1946:* Left Southampton for Jersey on resumption of peacetime service.
*1.1.1948:* Transferred to the British Transport Commission, London.
*12.1959:* Broken up at Nieuw Lekkerland, Netherlands by N.V. 'De Koophandel'.

## TONBRIDGE 1924-1941

O.N. 147690  682g 267n.
220.4 x 33.7 x 14.1 feet.
Two T.3-cyl. by D. and W. Henderson and Co. Ltd., Glasgow; 281 NHP, 1,850 IHP, 15 knots. Cargo capacity 30,340 cubic feet,
*3.6.1924:* Launched by D. and W. Henderson and Co. Ltd., Meadowside, Glasgow (Yard No. 633).
*10.7.1924:* Registered in the ownership of the Southern Railway Company, London as TONBRIDGE.

A post-war view of *Ringwood* (above). *[Ships in Focus]*

*18.7.1924:* Delivered at Southampton, for Strait of Dover services at a cost of £39,125.

*23.4.1927:* Damaged contacting the East Pier Head whilst entering Calais due to her inability to counteract strong running tide.

*14.2.1936:* In collision with the AUTOCARRIER outside Calais.

*18.11.1936:* Sustained further damage at Calais.

*23.3.1938:* In collision with the Boulogne breakwater.

*23.5.1940:* Left Folkestone for Southampton and St Malo to start new service to Plymouth.

*21.6.1940:* Left Guernsey with 250 women and children evacuees but required to wait 30 hours outside Weymouth.

*28.6.1940:* Arrived Southampton from Guernsey.

*28.8.1940:* Taken up for naval service as a netlayer.

*27.11.1940:* Commissioned as HMS TONBRIDGE.

*24.4.1941:* Left Falmouth for service in the North Sea.

*10.5.1941:* Escaped damage when attacked by German aircraft off the Humber.

*22.8.1941:* When returning to Great Yarmouth after laying obstructions off Sheringham, one bomb from an attacking German aircraft exploded between her funnel and bridge, whilst a second penetrated her mess deck aft, with the result that she sank by the head with the loss of 32 lives.

*23.3.1945:* Register closed.

## WHITSTABLE 1925-1959

O.N. 148656  687g 270n.
220.6 x 33.7 x 14.2 feet.
Cargo capacity 30,043 cubic feet.
Two T.3-cyl. by D. and W. Henderson and Co. Ltd., Glasgow: 281 NHP, 1,850 IHP, 15 knots.

*23.6.1925:* Launched by D. and W. Henderson and Co. Ltd., Meadowside, Glasgow (Yard No. 707).

*8.8.1925:* Registered in the ownership of the Southern Railway Company, London as WHITSTABLE.

*16.8.1925:* Delivered at Southampton at a cost of £41,450 for Strait of Dover services.

*1.5.1929:* Introduced a new service for cars from Folkestone.

*16/17.9.1935:* Moorings parted and lost 60 feet of belting in a severe gale whilst alongside the Prince of Wales Pier at Dover.

*10.12.1935:* Beltings further damaged during bad weather at Dover.

*29.5.1940:* Taken up for military service.

*31.5.1940:* Anchored close inshore off Bray beach, near Dunkirk, for over six hours under severe bombardment but only 14 soldiers available for rescue.

*Tonbridge* (above and middle) was one of the pre-war stalwarts of the Southern Railway Strait of Dover cargo service: in 1937 she made 385 Channel crossings and steamed more than 10,000 miles. *[National Maritime Museum P21177, World Ship Society Ltd.]*

*5.6.1940:* Left Dover for Southampton.

*12.6.1940:* Left Southampton, via Plymouth, under orders for Quiberon Bay, near St Nazaire, for possible troop evacuations but not used.

*21.6.1940:* Left Jersey for Weymouth with civilian evacuees.

*26.6.1940:* Released.

*28.6.1940:* Arived Plymouth from Jersey with a cargo of potatoes and laid up.

*11.3.1941:* Taken up for service as a Military Store Ship in the Irish Sea.

*21.3.1941:* Deckhouse badly damaged by incendiary bombs at Plymouth.

*21.10.1941:* Left Preston for six weeks' service between Penzance and the Scilly Isles.

*3.1.1942:* Released for service between Fishguard and Rosslare.

*30.1.1942:* Damaged port lifeboat and davit in collision with motor coaster ALACRITY (554/1940) at Rosslare.

*Whitstable* post-war. *[J. and M. Clarkson]*

*5.1942:* To Appledore for lay up.
*25.10.1942:* Assigned for further Irish Sea service.
*1.11.1943:* Allocated to Larne to Cairnryan milk service.
*6.3.1944:* In collision with HAMPTON FERRY (2,839/1934) in Loch Ryan.
*22.5.1944:* Assigned to the US Navy to carry salvage equipment and personnel.
*11.10.1944:* Left Cherbourg for Falmouth on completion of US service.
*1.1.1945:* Restarted on Larne to Cairnryan milk service.
*15.7.1945:* Released after refit at Manchester:
*17.7.1945:* Left Southampton for the Channel Islands on resumption of commercial service.
*27.11.1945:* Re-opened the Jersey to France service, sailing to Granville.
*6.6.1947:* Resumed cargo service from Dover.
*1.1.1948:* Transferred to the British Transport Commission, London (not registered until 21.7.1948).
*28.4.1959:* Arrived on the New Waterway for breaking up at Nieuw Lekkerland by N.V. 'De Koophandel'.

**WINCHESTER**
O.N. 182273  1,149g 424n 780d.
251.0 (l.o.a) 241.0 x 36.1 x 13.4 feet.
Cargo capacity 49,450 cubic feet.
2SCSA 10-cyl. (480 x 700mm) Sulzer-type oil engines by William Denny and Brothers Ltd., Dumbarton; 3,000 BHP, 16 knots.
*21.3.1947:* Launched by William Denny and Brothers Ltd., Dumbarton (Yard No. 1403).
*11.11.1947:* Delivered to the Southern Railway Company, London as WINCHESTER at a cost of £215,154 for Southampton services.
*1.1.1948:* Transferred to the British Transport Commission, London.
*1963:* Owners became the British Railways Board, London.
*1971:* Sold to Allied Finance S.A. (D.J. Chandris), Piraeus, Greece and renamed EXETER.
*1972:* Converted to a passenger vessel and renamed RADIOSA.
1987: Sold to Radiosa S.A. (Dominion International Services Inc.), Panama.
*2.7.1995:* Breaking up began at Myriknopoulos Shipyard, Perama by Ploiodilytiki Ltd.

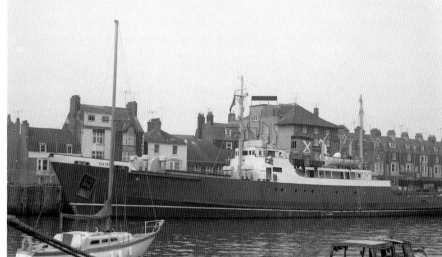

Top: Still looking impressive after 20 years, the 1947 *Winchester* is about to leave Jersey harbour. *[A.M.S. Russell collection]*

Middle: *Winchester* at Weymouth in her brief period with Chandris as *Exeter*. *[World Ship Society Ltd.]*

Lower middle: *Winchester* ended her days in Greek waters, much rebuilt as the excursion vessel *Radiosa*. *[David Whiteside collection]*

Bottom: Funnel and houseflag of the Southern Railway. *[J. L. Loughran]*

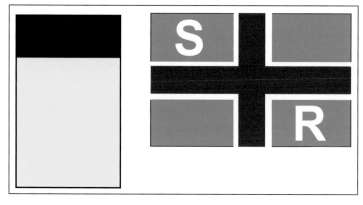

210

# BANK LINE: THE FINAL YEARS
## Malcolm Cranfield

A detailed review by Paul Boot of the post-war development of Bank Line's cargo ships, focusing on their design and aesthetics, appeared in 'Record' 17 and 18. Although trading routes were not described in his article, the concluding paragraph commented that Andrew Weir's Bank Line was still in existence, maintaining a regular service to the South Pacific Islands using four former Russian ro-ro ships which had been acquired in 1995 and adapted for that service.

In 2002 Bank Line's owners, Andrew Weir Shipping (AWS), made the decision to sell its Macandrews, United Baltic and Ellerman cargo liner businesses, retaining only Bank Line's South Pacific service. AWS also retained responsibility for the cargo/passenger vessel *St. Helena* (6,767/1990), handling both the commercial and technical management on behalf of the St. Helena Government. In the same year AWS won a contract from Foreland Shipping for the operation and technical management of six new ro-ro ships as part of a consortium including Bibby Line Group, Houlder and James Fisher PLC, each with a 25 per cent share. Then, in August 2003, John Swire and Sons Ltd.'s China Navigation Company acquired Bank Line's remaining service to the South Pacific; the four ships employed on it, however, remaining under AWS ownership and management. This article reviews in detail Bank Line's final trading routes, concluding with the South Pacific services, and the ships which were employed.

### Bank Line's routes
Post-war, Calcutta remained the most important centre for employment of the Bank Line fleet, their ships loading there for East Africa, South Africa, West Africa, the River Plate and the West Coast of South America. However, the trade from United States Gulf ports to Australia and New Zealand grew in significance while the long-established Pacific Islands to Europe service was resumed after the Pacific war. Tramping and chartering ships out to other cargo liner operators also provided important employment.

By the second half of the 1970s Bank Line's services were mostly centred on the US Gulf with separate sailings to and from UK/Continent, South Africa and outwards only to Australia and New Zealand, the ships returning to the USA and North Europe via the South Pacific Islands, by then known as the SoPac Service.

A return service from Australia and New Zealand to the US Gulf was started in 1977 with the creation of Bank and Savill Line for which the *Willowbank* and two near sisters were delivered in 1980. When this line was sold to the Shipping Corporation of New Zealand (SCONZ) in March 1984, *Willowbank* was chartered by SCONZ to operate on their ANCL, later ANZCL (Australia, New Zealand Container Line) or Boomerang service, to California until sold at Sydney in July 1988 to the Vestey Group. The sale had followed the 1988 merger of ANZCL with PAD (Pacific Australia Direct Line) to form ANZDL (Australia New Zealand Direct Line) and the subsequent sale of the SCONZ share in ANZDL to Sofrana Line (SOciété FRAnçaise de Navigation). The Auckland-based shipping arm of the Sofrana Group, Sofrana Unilines (NZ) Ltd, continues to operate services in the South Pacific.

*Willowbank* was built in 1980 by Smith's Dock, Middlesbrough for the Bank and Savill Line service between Australasia and the US Gulf, which ended in 1984. She is seen at Auckland on 27th January 1986 while running to the West Coast of the USA on charter to the Shipping Corporation of New Zealand. She was sold to the Vestey Group in 1988 and renamed *Mandowi* for operation by Austasia Line. Renamed *California Star* in 1989, she continued trading for Vestey until sold in 1996 to Pacific International Lines as *Sea Elegance*. From 2003 to 2008 she ran as *Golden Gate* before being beached at Alang on 23rd January 2009 to be broken up. *[Chris Howell collection]*

In 1979, for the first time, a service was introduced between United Kingdom and North Continental ports and the US Gulf using chartered-in, container-friendly tonnage: *Teakbank*, ex-*Hans Krüger* (in 1979), *Testbank*, ex-*Charlotta* (1979 to 1981), *Tielbank* ex-*Carolina* (1979 to 1981) and

*Tynebank*, launched as *Sandra Wesch* (1979 to 1980), which all used Cawoods' container terminal at Ellesmere Port on the Manchester Ship Canal. They were followed in 1981 by *Tynebank* ex-*Keta Lagoon*, which loaded at Felixstowe.

The first ship chartered by Bank Line for a new UK/North Continent to US Gulf service in 1979 was the *Hans Kruger*, the lead ship of the Neptun 401 type, built at Rostock in 1976. Renamed *Teakbank*, she is seen passing Eastham Ferry on 8th March 1979 outbound from Ellesmere Port on the Manchester Ship Canal (above). The charter finished at Hamburg in December 1979. The ship was broken up in India in 2002 as *Spica*. [Paul Boot]

Peter Döhle's 1978 Hamburg-built, 517-TEU capacity *Charlotta* and *Carolina* were both taken on charter by Bank Line in 1979 for two years and renamed *Testbank* and *Tielbank* respectively. *Testbank* is seen approaching Eastham Locks on 23rd May 1980 (middle) and *Tielbank* arriving at Rotterdam in August 1980 (bottom). *Charlotta* was sold in 1994 to Pacific International Lines to trade in the Far East as *Sri Manee* under the Thai flag, then from 1996 as *Sea Bright* under the Singapore flag, and was broken up at Chittagong in 2006. *Carolina* was sold in 1991 but survived for five years longer than her sistership, being beached at Alang in 2011 as the Syrian-owned *Nehad-D*. [ Author; Author's collection]

The newly-built, 590-TEU capacity *Sandra Wesch* was delivered at Kiel in November 1979 as *Tynebank* for charter to Bank Line. She is seen about to enter the Manchester Ship Canal on 8th May 1980. The charter finished in December 1980. Sold by Johnny Wesch to Ernst Komrowski in 1986 and renamed *Adrian*, she was beached at Alang in May 2007 as the UAE-owned *Yara*. *[Author]*

## East Asiatic Transpacific Service

Through their joint ownership of United Baltic Corporation (UBC) since 1919, AWS had forged strong links with East Asiatic Company (EAC) of Copenhagen. It is understood that EAC had been persuaded to take on charter, for two years from 1977, the 1973-built *Cloverbank*, renamed *Siena*, and the 1976-built *Firbank*, renamed *Sibonga*, in order to allow an evaluation of this Doxford ship design for employment on their United States to Far East services.

Unfortunately the service was rather disrupted by the ships frequently coming across, and taking on board, Vietnamese boat people. *Cloverbank* consequently came off-hire earlier than intended, in 1978, and EAC instead ordered from Nakskov a series of six ships of the Nakskov85 class which had a capacity of 542 TEU and were delivered in 1978 and 1979, including a new *Siena* (16,150/1979), with the last going to Pakistan as *Makran* (16,241/1979). But they also proved unsuitable as the trade soon became fully containerised, and EAC withdrew. In 1982 AWS bought out EAC's share in the United Baltic Corporation.

In 1977, the 1973-built *Cloverbank* and her 1976-built sister *Firbank* were taken on charter and renamed by the East Asiatic Company in order to allow an evaluation of this Doxford ship design for employment on their United States to Far East services. *Siena*, ex *Cloverbank,* is seen at Seattle in July 1978 (right) and *Sibonga*, ex *Firbank*, at San Francisco a month earlier (below), both with EAC funnel markings. *[Both: Author's collection]*

## SafBank

A pre-war service between the United States East Coast and Gulf ports and South Africa was re-launched by Bank Line in 1980 and, seeking to combat the threat posed by Mediterranean Shipping Company (MSC), a joint service with Safmarine, named SafBank Line, was started in 1987.

Bank Line had initially employed three of the new Fish-class ships built at Sunderland in 1978/9, *Tenchbank* and, briefly, *Ruddbank* and *Troutbank* which were soon replaced by *Roachbank* and *Dacebank*. However, by 1987 these ships, with a container capacity of only about 300 TEU, were proving inadequate and so were phased out of the service and the *Nara* and *Nausicaa*, built for Chargeurs Reunis, chartered in to replace them. *Nara* was renamed *Marabank* and *Nausicaa* became *Oakbank*. The charter of *Marabank* lasted only around one year, to be replaced by the chartered *Hazelbank* from early 1988 until the end of 1989. However, *Oakbank* continued on charter until 1990. *Nara* was then purchased by Bank Line and renamed *Olivebank*, replacing *Oakbank*, until sold in 1999. Meanwhile, *Dacebank* completed her last voyage from the USA around May 1987.

*Tenchbank*, completed by Sunderland Shipbuilders on 2nd November 1979, was photographed loading her first cargo at Hull for the Pacific Islands (above). In 1980 she re-opened Bank Line's service from United States East Coast and Gulf ports to South Africa. She was broken up at Alang in 2008 as *Multi Trader*. [Author's collection]

214

Entering service on 7th June 1979, *Ruddbank* is seen arriving at Rotterdam to load her first cargo, for China (opposite bottom), following which she briefly operated on the USA to South Africa service before returning to the charter market in 1981 (above). She was the first of the Fish class to be sold, going to Lamport and Holt Line at the end of 1983. Finally purchased by the ITF in 1998 and renamed *Global Mariner*, she sank in the Orinoco on 2nd August 2000 following a collision. *[Author's collection; FotoFlite incorporating Skyfotos 19511]*

SafBank Line was initially tonnaged by the 1977 Tønsberg-built *Nara* and the 1978 Oslo-built *Nausicaa*, both of which had recently been sold by their French owners Chargeurs Reunis. *Nara*, purchased by Mantica Holdings and managed by Wallem, was renamed *Marabank*. In 1990 she was purchased by Bank Line and renamed *Olivebank*, as seen in Safbank colours sailing from Durban. *[Russell Priest collection]*

215

Between 1989 and 1991 Safmarine operated two of their ships under Bank Line names and colours: *Rowanbank* (ex *Venture*, launched as *S.A. Venture)* and *Rosebank* (ex *Victory*, launched as *S.A. Victory*). When SafBank became fully containerised, Bank Line dropped out and Safmarine joined up with MSC.

**Oriental African Line**
Following the end of their employment on SafBank service in 1985 and 1986, *Tenchbank* and *Roachbank* had briefly joined *Troutbank* on the Far East to East/South Africa service, originally known as the Oriental African Line. An

agreement was then reached with Ahrenkiel to carry CKD (completely knocked down) automobiles from Japan to Port Elizabeth and hence *Tenchbank* was chartered to Ahrenkiel Liner Services as *ALS Strength* for about six months in mid-1986. Together with *Pikebank*, previously chartered out, *Tenchbank* then briefly rejoined Oriental African Line service until the ships were sold in September 1987.

The ten-year-old, 18.5-knot *Kassiakos*, renamed *Hazelbank,* was then chartered, but the service soon succumbed to competition and, as mentioned above, *Hazelbank* was transferred to SafBank service.

The Safmarine sisters operated on Safbank Line under Bank Line names, *Rowanbank* sails from Durban (upper) and *Rosebank* sails from Cape Town (lower). Renamed respectively *Stellenbosch* and *Algoa Bay* in 1993, they were beached at Alang on 28th September 2011 and 10th February 2012 for breaking up. *[Both: Trevor Jones]*

Entering service on 12th January 1979, *Roachbank* is seen arriving at Cape Town in May 1983 while on the USA to South Africa service (above). The limited container capacity of the Fish class led to her transfer to the Oriental Africa Line in 1986 and sale in 1987. As *Devo* she traded on until broken up at Haldia, India, in February 2001. *[Ian Shiffman/Author's collection]*

In 1987, the 1977 Tamano-built *Kassiakos* was taken on charter by Bank Line from Dioryx Maritime Corporation as *Hazelbank* for the Oriental Africa Line service (below). She had been built as *Amerika* for A/S Det Dansk-Franske Dampskibsselskab but was sold to Lemos and Pateras in 1979 to trade as *Thalassini Mana* until purchased by Dioryx at the end of 1987. When the

Oriental Africa Line service succumbed to competition she was transferred to the Safbank service for the balance of her two year charter. Subsequently chartered by Mediterranean Shipping Company, as *MSC Federica* between 1990 and 1993 and again as *MSC Sarah* between 1997 and 2002, *Kassiakos* was beached at Alang on 11th April 2003 for breaking. *[Trevor Jones]*

## SoPac

In 1989 Bank Line's eastbound service direct to Papua New Guinea via Suez was discontinued and replaced by a westabout, round-the-world service, tonnaged by the remaining four of the six *Corabank*-class ships. This was augmented by a joint service arrangement with Hamburg Süd's Columbus Line to which, between 1984 and 1986, and again in 1987, *Moraybank* was chartered and renamed

*Toana Papua* and in 1986/87, *Meadowbank* became *Toana Niugini*. Monthly sailings were offered from Hamburg, Hull, Antwerp, Dunkirk and Le Havre via the Panama Canal to Tahiti, the Pacific Islands, New Zealand, Papua New Guinea, Indonesia, Singapore, then returning to Europe via Suez.

In the mid 1990s the decision was made to invest in new tonnage. In 1995 four second-hand ships built in Finland between 1983-1985 to the Soviet standard SA15 type, known as the *Norilsk*-class, were purchased and flagged in the Isle of Man. The new ships were named *Foylebank* (ex-*Tiksi*), *Speybank* (ex-*Okha*), *Arunbank* (ex-*Bratsk*) and *Teignbank* (ex-*Nikel*). Each had a quarter ramp, useful to service ro/ro cargo at Auckland, and before entering service were fitted with bulbous bows, improved container capacity up to 576 TEU and heated deep-tanks for carrying up to 6,200 tons of coconut and vegetable/palm oil in bulk.

From August 2003 Swire managed the commercial operations, taking the ships on long-term charter from AWS who retained control of the passenger business, each ship having cabins available for 12 passengers. Swire took this step as the SoPac service had significant synergies with Swire's own managed trades in the region.

Swire then instigated a number of changes to the port rotation including calls in East Malaysia for plywood and nickel and in the Philippines for copra. Despite encroaching containerization in all major and secondary trade routes it was felt that a multipurpose service still made sense with numerous calls to relatively unsophisticated island ports and carrying basic bulks and neo-bulks such as copra, palm oil, lumber, coffee and cocoa beans on the homeward leg.

In 2006 China Navigation's liner trades were rebranded as Swire Shipping and the Bank Line name was phased out so that by 2007 the line became known as Swire Shipping's 'West-about Round the World Service' (WRTW). This complimented the counter-rotating 'East-about Round the World Service' between South

The *Norilsk* class vessel *Arunbank* is seen in the River Elbe on 20th September 1997 (above) while *Teignbank* was photographed passing Immingham, inbound for Hull, on 19th June 2000 (below). In 2006, when the ships were integrated into Swire Shipping's services, *Arunbank* was renamed *Tikeibank* and *Teignbank* became *Boularibank*. Both were broken up at Chittagong late in 2009. *[Author's collection]*

Asia and the U.S. Gulf operated by four INDOTRANS vessels purchased from Oldendorff in 2004. Also in 2006, the four ships underwent a major refit and, in order to better reflect their South Pacific trades, were renamed *Gazellebank* (ex-*Foylebank*), *Mahinabank* (ex-*Speybank*), *Tikeibank* (ex-*Arunbank*) and *Boularibank* (ex-*Teignbank*). AWS retained vessel ownership and technical management, in 2007 changing the ships' registry to Antigua and Barbuda.

In an effort to maintain schedule integrity Swire also chartered a sister ship from the Far East Shipping Company of Russia, *Anatoliy Kolesnichenko* (18,574/1985). Swire had also chartered *Vasiliy Burkhanov* (17,910/1986) for Chief Container Lines' trans-Tasman service.

Unfortunately, due to weak markets in the United States and Europe, the former Bank Line round the world service ended in July 2009 with the sailing from Europe of *Mahinabank*, ending over 100 years of operation on this route. Swire Shipping has since offered to customers their Europe Pacific Express, utilising global container line services between Europe and Singapore where containers are transhipped to the Pacific Islands, Australia and New Zealand with on carriage connections to all major ports in Papua New Guinea and the Solomon Islands.

*Mahinabank*, formerly *Speybank* and *Okha,* was photographed arriving at Hamburg on 4th July 2009 for the last sailing from Europe to the Pacific Islands. She was beached at Chittagong on 2nd November 2009 for breaking. *[Aleksi Lindström ]*

*Anatoliy Kolesnichenko* (right) was taken on charter in 2007 for Swire's Europe Pacific Express service (the former Bank Line round the world service). Seen at Tauranga on 25th June 2008, she was beached at Chittagong on 26th July 2012 for breaking. *[David Pratt ]*

## PNG-South East Asia Service

In 1988 a joint service with Swire, known as ASPAC, commenced between Papua New Guinea and other Pacific islands, Singapore and South East Asia. Swire already had a service between South East Asia and the east coast of Australia via Papua New Guinea and it is thought that this new service was designed to give faster separate services to Papua New Guinea and the Australian ports.

Bank Line proceeded to charter from German owners for this service the 1977-built *Henriette Schulte*, renamed *Taybank*, and the 1983-built *Calabar*, renamed *Coralbank*. When both came off-hire in 1989, Swire proceeded to charter *Taybank* as *Nanchang* until 1991.

In 1993 the management of Swire's New Guinea Pacific Line (NGPL) moved from Hong Kong – via a three-year joint venture with Bank Line and Columbus Line in Singapore – to be consolidated with that of Chief Container Service (CCS) in the Swire Shipping offices in Sydney. With the initiation of a trans-Tasman service in 1999, Swire in Sydney also became a natural focus for management of these services.

In 1988 Bank Line took on charter as for the joint ASPAC service the *Henriette Schulte*, renaming her *Taybank*, as photographed at Singapore on 25th June 1989 (right). Swire soon took over the charter, renaming the ship *Nanchang*, until she went off hire in 1991. In the following year she was sold to China where she was broken up in 2011 as *Zhe Hai 325*. [Simon Olsen]

From 1996 *Forthbank*, together with *Clydebank*, was employed on the joint Bank-Ellerman service. Seen at Singapore, *Forthbank* was sold for further trading at Singapore in mid 2000 (below). As the Singapore-managed *Pacific Emerald*, she was beached at Chittagong on 16th December 2002 for breaking. [Chris Howell collection]

## Bank-Ellerman

Two of the *Corabank*-class ships displaced from the SoPac service in 1996, the *Clydebank* and *Forthbank*, were employed on a service between South Africa and the Arabian Gulf, Pakistan and India known as Bank-Ellerman. This was a monthly service from Durban with a round trip scheduled to last about 56 days calling at Dar-es-Salaam, Mombasa, Jebel Ali, Karachi and Mumbai, returning to Durban via Mombasa. The Ellerman name was only used as this was a deep-sea trade which had derived from former Ellerman services. The joint name had also helped to differentiate the service from the traditional Bank Line trades.

The ships were of the geared, 'tween-deck type, suitable for the carriage of a wide variety of cargoes such as bagged rice and spices, steel in various forms (coils, rods, plates and girders), forest products (e.g. paper, chipboard), second-hand cars and new safari coaches, plus a few containers.

In 1998, the 1977-built *Sea Exporter*, renamed *Ettrickbank*, was taken on time charter but the service did not prosper, the ship coming off hire in 1999. Early in 2000 *Clydebank* was sold to breakers while *Forthbank* was sold for further trading.

In 1998, the Hiroshima-built *Gregor*, owned by Ormos Cia. Nav. S.A. of Piraeus was taken on time charter for the Bank-Ellerman service and renamed *Ettrickbank*. As the service was unsuccessful, she came off hire without change of name, as pictured in December 1999. Early in 2000, placed under Dubai management, her name was shortened to *Rickbank*. Resold in 2005 to Bangladesh interests, she traded on as *Yaad-E-Mostafa* until beached at Alang on 17th December 2009 for breaking. *[Author's collection]*

## Tamahine Shipping

Bank Line's much admired ships have now all gone. One person who had a particular liking for them was Mark Bamford, owner of Tamahine Shipping, whose first purchase from Bank Line for further trading was the former *Maplebank*, built at Belfast in 1967, which had traded as *Kavo Yossonas* between 1979 and 1985. Renamed *Kowloon Countess*, after some difficulty in raising her anchor amidst a number of laid up ships, she sailed from Piraeus in May 1985 under the management of West Hartlepool Steam Navigation Co. Ltd. bound for Dunkirk to load a cargo of sugar for India. En route to Suez she called at Gibraltar where she was sold to shipbreaking intermediaries and, following discharge of her cargo, was beached near Karachi on 29th August 1985 to be broken up. This purchase had followed, early in 1983, the acquisition of the laid up *Newcrest*, the former *Ashbank*, with immediate resale to Spanish breakers, although the ship ran aground near Gijon on 7th February 1983 and was broken up in situ.

Seen arriving at Durban, *Maplebank* was purchased by Tamahine Shipping for further trading and renamed *Kowloon Countess* in 1985. Her career with Tamahine was woefully short, and later that year she was sold to breakers at Karachi following problems with her generators. *[Trevor Jones]*

Incidentally, the first ship purchased by Tamahine Shipping was the 1953-built *Tamasinga* (3,575/1953), placed under the nominal ownership of Titanic Salvage Co. Ltd. in the Cayman Islands. Built in Italy for Greek South American Line (Vernicos-Eugenides) as *Athinai* she was operated for two years from 1979 as *Googi Z.*, owned by the London-based Mithshina Shipping and Traders Ltd., until arriving at Barbados on 26th November 1980 in a damaged condition. It is reported that, when the ship was purchased by Tamahine, she was initially intended to be named *Tamahi 1* but sailed under tow a year later for breaking at Brownsville, Texas, as *Tamasinga*.

Tamahine's next purchase was the 1978 Sunderland-built *Crestbank*, purchased in mid-1986 and renamed *Tamathai* but immediately laid up in pristine condition at Birkenhead until resold to Greek owners later the following year to operate as *Northman*. Most unusually, she was re-purchased by Tamahine early in 1988 and renamed *Tamamima* as which she arrived at Immingham on 26th April to load for India. Sailing on 14th May 1988, she briefly grounded soon after sailing but was refloated without damage and traded successfully for ten years until laid up at Falmouth in July 1998.

Efforts to find a permanent home for *Tamamima* as a museum ship having failed, she was sold in 2005, narrowly avoiding a sale to breakers, to initially trade as *Berga* and then,

from 2006, as *Novanoor* until beached near Karachi on 20th February 2010 for breaking. Tamahine had in 2000 purchased the former buoy tender *Fingal* (1,342/1964) Renamed *Windsor Castle*, she was also laid up at Falmouth but sailed under tow on 14th August 2014 bound for Leith to become a floating hotel berthed next to the royal yacht *Britannia* (5,769/1954). *Windsor Castle* was donated by Mr. Bamford to The Royal Yacht Britannia Trust to be preserved.

The Greek owners of *Northman*, P. Apostolou and D.Benas, who had traded from 1986 as Transman Shipping Enterprises S.A., also went on to purchase the *Tenchbank*, renamed *Eastman*, only to sell the ship to Tamahine Shipping in 1989. Renamed *Tamathai*, in 1993 AWS was awarded a management contract for the ship but she was resold in 1995 and ended her days as *Multi Trader* at Alang in October 2008, some six years after all her sister ships had been broken up. Those same Greek owners had in 1987 also purchased *Pikebank*, renamed *Westman*, which traded continuously until beached at Alang on 9th January 2001 to be scrapped.

In 1991 the former *Ruddbank* was also purchased by Tamahine to trade as *Tamapatcharee*. In 1994 AWS was awarded a management contract for the ship but she was resold in 1995 to Hong Kong operators J. McRink and Co. and renamed *Lady Rebecca*. Purchased by the International Transport Federation in 1998 and renamed *Global Mariner*,

*Crestbank* was the last traditional Bank Line ship to be broken up, in 2010 as *Novanoor*. As *Tamamima* she was photographed transiting the Suez Canal on 19th June 1995 during a liner voyage from London to Aqaba (above). *[Author]*Transman Shipping Enterprises S.A. of Piraeus purchased a number of the Fish class ships including, in 1987, *Pikebank*. Renamed *Westman* she is seen passing Terneuzen, outbound from Antwerp, at dusk on 2nd June 2000 (above). *[Author]*

she was initially berthed at Bremen as an exhibition and training ship but resumed trading in 2000 only to sink in the Orinoco River on 2nd August that year following a collision.

Tamahine went on to purchase two sister ships built by Scotts at Greenock in 1980 for the Ocean Group. In 1994 the former *Myrmidon* (16,482/1980) became *Tamamonta*, which traded until beached at Alang in January 2002 for breaking, and in 1995 the former *Mentor* (16,482/1980) which became *Tamatiki*, trading until beached at Alang in May 2001.

## The end of the Fish-class
The first vessel to be sold was *Ruddbank* which, operated on the charter market since 1981, was positioned to the UK by loading a cargo of bulk sugar cane at Mauritius for London in October 1983. Purchased by Lamport and Holt and renamed *Romney* at Rotterdam, she proceeded to load several cargoes at Avonmouth for the Falklands, each time returning to the UK from Brazil on the BRISA service, discharging at Liverpool.

On expiry of the Falklands contract in the summer of 1986, *Romney* was repositioned to the South Pacific, via Karachi, to operate on Vestey's cargo liner service to the West Coast of USA/Canada. Initially renamed *Lairg* under the nominal ownership of Highvale Ltd. of London, a company created by Wallem in 1984, and management of Lion Shipping Ltd. of Hong Kong, so sporting a lion shape on her funnel, she was renamed *Napier Star* in 1989. Her career after sale in 1991, together with those of *Tenchbank* and *Pikebank*, is described above, and photographs will be found in the latest Ships in Focus book, 'Blue Star: A Fleet History'.

Of the remaining three ships sold in 1987, *Dacebank* was purchased by N. and E. Leondaras (Leond Maritime) of Piraeus. As the *Anna L.* she had visited Liverpool in February 1988 on voyage charter to T. and J. Harrison and between 1991 and 1994 was taken on time charter by Blue Star Line as *Washington Star*. She was sold to other Greek operators in 1997 and finished her career

*Napier Star*, the former *Ruddbank,* sailing from Vancouver on 13th June 1990. [Chris Howell collection]

Entering service on 23rd June 1979, *Dacebank* was sold in 1987. As the *Anna L.* she visited Durban in July 1988 during a voyage from India to South America (right). [Trevor Jones]

under Hong Kong management as *Bute* during 2001/2, being beached at Alang in October 2002 for breaking.

    The identity of the buyers of *Roachbank*, renamed *Devo* at Yokohama, and *Troutbank*, renamed *Brij* at Kobe, is unclear. Initially managed by Aegeus Shipping of Piraeus, who had also managed the Fafalios fleet including several former Bank Line ships, their management was soon transferred to Trishul Ship Management of New York. By 1995 the ships were managed, and it seems owned, by Sinha Shipping Private Ltd. of Bombay for whom *Devo* traded continuously until sold for breaking in 2001 while *Brij* was sold for further trading in 1999 and broken up in 2002 as *Accord I*.

**Conclusion**

Having been laid up in good condition by Tamahine Shipping for several years, *Crestbank* was the last traditional Bank Line ship to be broken up, in 2010, 18 months after the former *Tenchbank*, while the last *Corabank*-class ship to be scrapped was *Ivybank*, in 2003 after five years under the ownership of Peter Cremer's Pro Line as *Pro Pacifica*.

    It is believed that the only ship still in operation which once had a Bank Line name, albeit not a traditional one, is the former chartered-in *Coralbank* as the Kuwait-owned *Lady Haluom*.

The former *Dacebank*, time chartered by Blue Star Line as *Washington Star* between 1991 and 1994, is seen in the Fraser River, Western Canada, on 21st August 1993 (above). *[Marc Piché]*

The 1987 buyers of the *Roachbank*, renamed *Devo*, are thought to be Indian. The photographs show *Devo* at Mersin on 25th March 1989 whilst operated by Trishul Ship Management (right upper) and at Singapore post-1995 in Sinha Shipping ownership (right lower). *[Hans Hoffmann; Gerhard Fiebiger]*

*Brij*, the former *Troutbank*, is seen arriving at Rotterdam on 11th January 1989 at the end of a voyage from the west coast of South America whilst she was managed by Trishul Ship management. Sold for further trading in 1999, it is believed to other Indian principals, she briefly traded as *Alim*, managed by Brighton Shipping Corporation of Watford, before becoming *Accord 1*, managed by Marine Management Services of Kingston-upon-Thames. She was beached at Alang on 24th April 2002 for breaking. *[Hans Hoffmann]*

During 1986/7 *Meadowbank* was renamed *Toana Niugini* for a joint service to the Pacific islands with Columbus Line whose colours she wore. Photographed outbound from Antwerp on 3rd October 1986 bound for Lae, she briefly reverted to the name *Meadowbank* before being sold in 1988 to trade as *Pro Atlantica* until arriving at Zhangjiagang on 11th July 2000 to be broken up. *[Markus Berger]*

At the time of writing the only ship still in existence which had a Bank Line name is *Lady Haluom*, seen off Misurata, Libya, on 22nd July 2012. Formerly the chartered-in *Coralbank*, she was built at Flensburg in 1983 as the German-owned *Calabar* and since 2009 has been owned by the Kuwait-domiciled Al-Bahar Shipping Limited. *[Muhsen Hussein]*

Mentioned in the opening paragraph is the continuing management by AWS of the vessel *St. Helena*. By way of background, the island of St. Helena in the South Atlantic Ocean was until 1977 served by ships of the Union Castle Line. The 1963 Canadian built cargo/passenger ship *Northland Prince* was then purchased and renamed *St. Helena,* managed by Curnow Shipping of Porthleven, Cornwall, with the intention that she served the island from Cape Town. However, this ship, which incidentally was used by the Royal Navy during the Falklands War as a minesweeper support ship, when she was temporarily replaced by Blue Funnel Line's *Centaur*, proved to be too small.

A new purpose-built *St. Helena* was therefore ordered from Hall, Russell and Company in Aberdeen, entering service in October 1990. The old *St. Helena* was meantime briefly renamed *St. Helena Island* while continuing in operation pending the new ship entering service. The new *St Helena* is equipped to carry a wide range of cargo, including liquids and livestock, with berths for 128 passengers, a swimming pool, shop and well-equipped medical facilities. The ship's capacity was extended in 2012 by the addition of 24 extra cabin berths and a gymnasium.

In 2001 the management contract for the ship's commercial and technical operations was awarded to AWS and the ship currently remains in service although an airport on the island is now being built, scheduled to be open in 2016.

Photographed at Gibraltar on 3rd December 2005, *Indotrans Flores* is relevant to the Bank Line story in so far as she was employed by Swire in a complementary round-the-world service to the one in which the former Soviet Bank Line ships were employed. In 2004 Swire had purchased four sister ships built in 1984 for Leif Høegh and which had passed to Egon Oldendorff in 2001. Renamed by Swire in 2006, they were all broken up in China during 2012, two of the ships having been given traditional Swire names shortly before sale. Thus *Indotrans Flores* very briefly traded as *Hupeh*. [Daniel Ferro]

The 1963 Canadian-built *St. Helena*, which had operated services to the Island from 1977 to 1990, is seen at Avonmouth under the name *St. Helena Island* which she had been briefly given during 1990 (opposite middle). Blue Funnel Line's *Centaur* (7,989/1964), seen sailing from Cape Town in December 1982 (opposite bottom), had substituted for her during 1982/3. The 1989 Aberdeen-built *St. Helena* is seen sailing from Cardiff on 12th May 1994 (above) and in dry dock at Cape Town in August 2006 (right). *[P.W. Hobday; Trevor Jones; Nigel Jones; Ian Shiffman]*

**Bank Line owned or chartered ships mentioned in text**
Former and later names plus year of build and grt as built or acquired.

*Arunbank* (18,627/1983) ex-*Bratsk* later *Tikeibank*
*Ashbank* (8,694/1959) later *Newcrest*
*Cloverbank* (11,452/1973) later *Siena*
*Clydebank* (11,405/1974)
*Corabank* (11,405/1973) later *Unicosta*
*Coralbank* (5,500/1983) ex *Calabar*, later *Lady Haluom*
*Crestbank* (11,238/1978) later *Tamathai, Northman Tamamima, Berga* and *Novanoor*
*Dacebank* (12,214/1979) later *Anna L, Washington Star* and *Bute*
*Ettrickbank* (13,542/1977) ex *Sea Exporter*, ex *Gregor*, later *Rickbank, Yaad-e-Mostafa*
*Firbank* (11,282/1976) later *Sibonga*
*Forthbank* (11,405/1973) later *Pacific Emerald*
*Foylebank* (18,627/1983) ex-*Tiksi*, later *Gazellebank*
*Hazelbank* (14,545/1977) ex-*Amerika*
*Ivybank* (11,405/1974) later *Pro Pacifica*
*Maplebank* (10,365/1967) later *Kavo Yossonas* and *Kowloon Countess*
*Marabank* (16,893/1977) ex-*Nara*, later *Olivebank*

*Meadowbank* (11,405/1973) later *Toana Niugini, Pro Atlantica*
*Moraybank* (11,405/1973) later *Toana Papua*
*Oakbank* (16,893/1978) ex-*Nausicaa*
*Olivebank* (16,893/1977) ex-*Nara*, ex-*Marabank*
*Pikebank* (12,214/1979) later *Westman*
*Roachbank* (12,214/1979) later *Devo*
*Rosebank* (18,297/1978) ex- *Victory*, launched as *S.A. Victory*
*Rowanbank* (18,575/1978) ex- *Venture,* launched as *S.A. Venture*
*Ruddbank* (12,214/1979) later *Romney,Tamapatcharee, Lady Rebecca* and *Global Mariner*
*Speybank* (18,627/1983) ex-*Okha*, later *Mahinabank*
*Taybank* (8,580/1977) ex-*Henriette Schulte*, later *Nanchang*
*Teakbank* (9,019/1976) ex-*Hans Krüger*
*Teignbank* (18,627/1984) ex-*Nikel*, later *Boularibank*
*Tenchbank* (12,214/1979) later *ALS Strength, Eastman, Tamathai,* and *Multi Trader*
*Testbank* (9,313/1978) ex-*Charlotta*
*Tielbank* (9,310/1978) ex-*Carolina*
*Troutbank* (12,214/1979) later *Brij* and *Accord I*
*Tynebank* (13,004/1980) ex-*Keta Lagoon*
*Tynebank* (8,193/1979) launched as *Sandra Wesch*
*Willowbank* (17,789/1980) later *Mandowi, California Star, Sea Elegance* and *Golden Gate*

Chris Gee kindly sent photographs he took in Hong Kong on 12th June 1981 of two ships recently featured in 'Record'. Mentioned on page 121 and 122 of 'Record' 58 was *Caesarea* (4,174/1960), seen above caught in the act of becoming *Aesarea*: note the crew member painting out the letter C on the stern. She was broken up in 1992. Stan Zapiec notes that the photo of *Caesarea* in 'Record' 58 was not taken in Weymouth but in the Channel Islands, possibly St Helier.

Anchored near to *Aesarea* in Hong Tong was what Chris describes as a rather scruffy Chinese ship, *Lu Hai 65* (6,997/1958), which was formerly the *Yang-Tse* of Messageries Maritimes, which was featured on page 21 in 'Record' 57. *Lu Hai 65* left the Chinese register in 1993, presumably scrapped. *[Both: Chris Gee]*

East Indiaman *Atlas* 1813

Royal Mail Ship *Britannia* 1840

Tea Clipper *Cutty Sark* 1870

Cargo Liner *Clan Matheson* 1919

Royal Mail Ship *Queen Elizabeth* 1940

Bulk Carrier *Lord Hinton* 1986

**Ships on stamps**

Mention of *Lord Hinton* in the editorial of 'Record' 55 prompted reader Michael Dick to send the stamps shown here, which were issued by the Royal Mail on 19th September 2013. The issue coincided with the 70th anniversary celebrations of the Battle of the Atlantic. It is refreshing to see that, whilst some old favourites are shown, including *Queen Elizabeth* of 1940 and *Cutty Sark* of 1870, the set has at least three ships which are not particularly well known: the East Indiaman *Atlas* of 1813, the cargo liner *Clan Matheson* of 1919 and the collier *Lord Hinton* of 1986. It is interesting to note that all except the East Indiaman, which was built near Hull, were constructed on the Clyde.

# JAPANESE SURVIVOR

Chris Gee has sent the accompanying photographs of *Wing On* (1.972/1940), working timber in the Western Anchorage at Singapore on 4th March 1978. The 38-year-old motor ship is particularly interesting as she is one of the last survivors of a Japanese standard design, the D class, the first of 85 of which was built in 1936. Over time their appearance altered but they retained the same basic profile. During the war they were frequently mistaken for tankers which meant they suffered a higher level of attack. The long raised quarterdeck hatches made them ideal for carrying military equipment including landing barges and they served in all theatres of the Pacific War.

*Wing On* at Singapore, 4th March 1978. *[Chris Gee]*

*Wing On* was completed in February 1940 as *Mishima Maru* by Tsurumi Saitetsu Zosen, Yokohama who also built her triple-expansion steam engine. Almost all of the Ds were sunk during the war, the *Mishima Maru* being no exception as she was mined and sunk on 15th May 1945 near Okinoshima, Ehime Ken in position 34.30 north, 135.10 east with the loss of one crew member. She was raised after the war and was back in service as *Mishima Maru* by August 1949, and was re-engined with a Japanese diesel in 1964. Subsequent names were *Lisana* in 1967, *Arana* in 1968, and *Angelina* in 1969, all under the Panama flag. Chris's photo shows her soon after renaming *Wing On* and probably after a recent dry-docking in view of the condition of her hull, boot-topping, and painted draft marks. Owners were Straits Chartering and Agencies Ltd., Singapore but she was registered at Amapala, Honduras. Unfortunately on 28th May 1978 just under three months after being photographed she sprang a leak and was abandoned by her crew (who were rescued) in the Bay of Bengal in position 11.36 north, 83.35.30 east during a voyage from Madras to Muara, Brunei with barytes.

As *Lisana* and *Angelina*, she was photographed by others at Singapore (see below), but Chris's photographs of her as *Wing On* may well be unique, given her short life under this name.

The editors would like to thank both Chris for the excellent photographs, and Peter Cundall, an Australian expert on Japanese shipping, for information for the caption.

*Wing On* at Singapore, 4th March 1978. *[Chris Gee]*

*Wing On* under previous her names, *Lisana* (upper) and *Angelina* (lower), the latter at Singapore 14th March 1976. Under both names she was registered in Panama for companies managed by Ednasa Co. Ltd., Hong Kong. *[V.H. Young and L.A. Sawyer; Chris Gee]*

# PUBLISHERS' PICK
## Roy Fenton and John Clarkson

Every tenth issue of 'Record', the editors are lct out from behind their computers, remove their eye-shades and are allowed to select for the bonus colour pages a few images taken during what passed for their youth. Each photograph is chosen because it shows an unusual occurrence or because it has a story attached. Or just because an editor likes it.

### Ellerman exposure
Birkenhead Docks were in cycling distance of the photographer's home, offering a mix of cargo liners, tramps and ore carriers which made it an education for a teenage ship spotter. Motor transport was available in 1973 when the *City of Leeds* (7,622/1950) was photographed on 12th August (above). The former *City of Ottawa* remained with Ellerman until 1975, after which she spent two years as *Gulf Venture* before reaching Gadani Beach. For more about her career, see 'Record' 21, 27 and 46. *[Roy Fenton 164/22]*

### Iron exchange
The John Summers' steel works on Deeside required regular replenishments of iron ore, brought into Birkenhead's Bidston Dock then railed to Shotton. Saturday 12th October 1975 saw a changeover of ore carriers, with the Liberian *Weser Ore* (8,208/1959) locking out into the Mersey (upper), and the arrival of the Italian *Giovanni Agnelli* (11,258/1956) on the same tide, and with the same fine autumnal lighting (lower). In 1976 the Liberian went on to become a US-

owned offshore mining vessel before being scrapped in China in 1993. The Italian ore carrier was also sold in 1976,

becoming *Evaki*, and was demolished at Kaohsiung three years later. *[Roy Fenton 181/29 and 181/36]*

## Eastham encounters

East Coast colliers were unknown in the North West until they began to become redundant in the 1960s, after which even the occasional up-river collier or 'flat-iron' turned up. One of the larger conventional types built to serve a gas works well down river, in her case that at East Greenwich, was the former *Catford* seen leaving the Manchester Ship Canal as *Oliva* (2,724/1948) on 4th April 1970. Since the South Eastern Gas Board sold her in 1967 she had carried the names *Aispiros*, *Zephyros* and *Point Clear*. *Oliva* was her last, and as this she sank off Jutland on 8th July 1971 following an engine room fire and explosion during a voyage from Szczecin to Leith with a cargo of chemicals. *[Roy Fenton]*

Apart from the then-annual CWS cruise in a Mersey ferry, passenger shipping on the Manchester Ship Canal was unknown. So the visit by *Balmoral* (688/1949) to the Boat Museum at Ellesmere Port on 3rd July 1978 was a memorable occasion. It was probably even more unforgettable for her master or pilot, as the *Balmoral* seemed very difficult to control. She entered the lock at Eastham at an angle of about 30 degrees, and the steering problem recurred as, when revisited an hour or so later at Ellesmere Port, *Balmoral* was moored at a similar angle. *Balmoral* is still with us, although currently laid up. *[Roy Fenton]*

## Good morning Garston

Whilst photographing at Eastham, ships can be seen way across the Mersey Estuary, creeping into or out of Garston. But just as the sun is perfectly positioned for photography at Eastham from morning onwards, for ships off Garston it is perfectly wrong. Only in summer on an early tide is the light right, and such a day was chosen in May 1988 and the alarm clock set. A lengthy drive was rewarded by absolutely nothing stirring, but the following morning there was compensation.

Outward was something of a rarity for the time, the Turkish-built and owned coaster *Ayca* (1,533/1984). Her career has gone almost full circle, and after a variety of owners she is back in Turkey, albeit under the flag of St Vincent and the Grenadines, as *Seher Yildizi*.

The photographer has yet to see other shots taken from the same vantage point, the 'Iron Shore' at Otterspool. Are there any out there? *[Roy Fenton 415/14]*

## Lasting Latvian

The latter part of the DFDS route from Harwich to Hamburg, with its long cruise up the River Elbe, provided a feast of photographic opportunities, before the service was cut back to Cuxhaven and finally withdrawn altogether. On 18th September 1977 the Latvian-registered tanker *Riga* (12,588/1967) was passed in the lower reaches of the Elbe  Her classic, bridge-amidships profile was notable even in the late 1970s, and would be even more unusual by 1993 when she went to breakers at Alang. *[Roy Fenton 30/204]*

## Survivor snapped

One of the last chances to snap a classic cargo liner came when the *Indian Endurance* (10,016/1975) approached the locks at Antwerp on 8th April 1990. Built in India, and broken up there in 1996, she had the distinction of going to the breakers under the name with which she started life. *[Roy Fenton 464/14]*

## Winter on the Waterway

Of many hundreds of shots taken on the Nieuw Waterweg, this one has been chosen for its dramatic lighting.  The banks of this waterway can be coolish even in summer, but on this occasion it was worth braving the December 1990 weather as the low, afternoon light lit up an ordinary coastal tanker, the Swedish *Margot* (449/1966), against darkening trees and sky.  At almost 40 years old, she is still around, working as a bunkering tanker under the Russian flag as *Natalya Goncharova*.
*[Roy Fenton 495/4]*

Like Roy, Eastham was one of my favourite places for photography as it offered a wide variety of shipping as seen on this page. Advantages over Liverpool were the movements were concentrated over a few hours rather than throughout the day, no photography permit was required and the ships passed you rather than having to travel between various lock entrances - a great advantage as one got older.

Everard's tankers such as *Alignity* (890/1945) (above left) were regular visitors to the Ship Canal loading various oils for other ports and sometimes bunker fuel for ships in Liverpool or Birkenhead. In the 1970s it was rare not to see at least one decent sized tanker such as Common Brothers *Border Falcon* (13,238/1961) (above right) going in or out of the canal or oil dock.

Sailing from the canal is *Vickers Voyager* (3,004/1959) (below left). After arriving in the canal as the factory trawler *Fairtry II* she had been converted into a research ship at Manchester Dry Docks. *Trecarne* (6,499/1959) (below right) with pristine paintwork and in Hain-Nourse colours had obviously already been in drydock when she was photographed on 3rd July 1969 approaching Eastham.

As mentioned above Liverpool and Birkenhead were not regular ports for me but calling in at Birkenhead one Saturday on my way to Eastham, I managed to photograph *Atlantic Ocean* (6,049/1962) (right), formerly *Clan Finlay* sailing partially loaded.

Over the years I mainly photographed in black and white but from time to time took a few colour pictures. The first colour slide I ever took was *Linda Dan* (1,593/1936) sailing from Preston (below left). The camera was an Ilford Sportsman, never intended for serious photography, but the result is passable if not blown up too much. Another from the early days was *Cristo* (143/1916) seen swinging in the dock basin at Preston prior to going port side to on the stone berth.

Starting in the mid-1950s Preston became a busy container port serving various ports in Ireland. One of the early ships, *Loch Linnhe* (753/1928) (top left) is seen arriving at Preston,. She was certainly not built for the job and carried only 20 to 30 containers or flats. H.M.Thomson's *Sithonia* (7,213/1942) (above right and right), formerly *Ocean Volga*, arrived at Preston on 18th December 1961 for breaking up. It was a great surprise cycling across the dock to work to see this large ship, for Preston, which had appeared overnight. Ward's men must have turned out to meet her as when photographed at 8am a slit had already been cut in the hull to put mooring ropes into the chain locker. *Sithonia* was the last decent sized vessel scrapped at Preston.

At one time Everard's tankers were regular visitors to Lancaster with linseed oil for the linoleum works but the only ship I ever saw there was *Clyde Valley* (476/1886) ex *Londoner*, ex *Balniel*. After many years service in Canada she was brought back to Carrickfergus, Ireland and then to Lancaster in 1974, with plans for preservation (far right). Unfortunately these came to nothing and she was cut up *in situ*.

Glasson Dock was ideal for small coasters such as the Ramsey registered *Sulby River* (196/1971) (right) which operated a service to the Isle of Man. Outside the dock and behind the pub was a berth used for long lay-ups, shipbreaking etc. *King Orry* (2,485/1946) was laid up there for some time but in January 1976 during a severe storm she broke away, drifted upstream and onto the marshes (bottom right) She lay there until April 1976 when she was refloated and towed back to her berth.

*Holland XXIV* (bottom left) was brought to Blackpool in 1981 to replenish and raise the beach by pumping sand ashore. In a winter gale she broke adrift and went ashore. The pipe used for pumping sand ashore was badly damaged and orange coloured polystyrene lagging, used to keep the pipe afloat, littered the beaches for miles.

Visits to Heysham were infrequent, generally only following a tip off about something out of the usual, such as the Lebanese *Byblos*

(2,725/1970) (above left) leaving port after discharging Cyprus potatoes. Whilst there one always took the opportunity to photograph

any other ships on the move, in this case Sealink Manx Line's ro-ro ferry *Manx Viking* (3,589/1976) (above right) in Sealink colours.

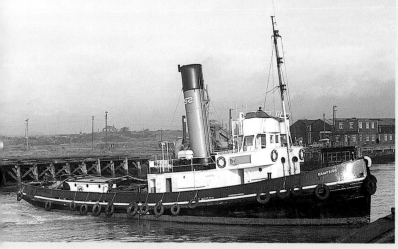

My first visit to Barrow was about 1970 to look after a Geest Line ship discharging there and I took the opportunity to photograph the local tugs including *Rampside* (240/1941) the former *Empire Fir* (above left). In 1972 I went back, this time to photograph HMS *Tyne* awaiting demolition but more interesting, and a surpise, were the remains of the trawler *Stephill* which had been lost near Barrow. The wreck had to be lifted to facilitate dredging operations and a crane *Taklift*

*I* was brought in. Once lifted the crane carried the trawler into dock, depositing it on spare ground where she is seen in the early stages of demolition.

Millom was a much longer journey and only made for special ships. On 13th July 1986 Marion and I went there to photograph the former Preston tug *Frank Jamieson* (146/1956) said to have recently arrived for scrapping. All we could find was the hull of the Maryport Maritime Museum's tug *Torque* (229/1943) (below left) from

which almost everything, including engines, had been removed. Her funnel on the quayside was the only other recognisable piece (below right). Of *Frank Jamieson* there was no sign until Marion had a closer look at a pile of scrap (bottom right) and our search was ended.

Other than Merseyside the north west never had the quantity of shipping found elsewhere in England but over the years it was always woirth getting out and about to see what one could find.

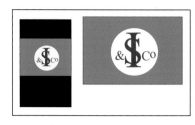

Coal exporting; tramp ships; distributing and mining coal; airliners and back to coasters: few ship owners had such a varied range of business interests as the Instone family.

Born in 1878 in Gravesend as Samuel Einstein, Samuel Instone first became a significant player in the coal export business in Cardiff, also setting up import and distribution companies in France and Italy, and buying ships and later collieries as an adjunct to his earlier businesses. He quickly recognised the opportunities which the outbreak of war in 1914 provided, and had the blessing of the establishment in profitable time charters of neutral shipping. However, his judgement let him down in ambitious ventures which could have made him a major ship owner. Nevertheless, thanks to the resilience of his other businesses, Instone survived. Indeed, he must be one of the few owners of tramp ships to have begun an airline, and the only one to have a village named after him.

## Into business
Samuel Instone moved to Cardiff probably in 1899 where he became a manager for Compagnie Maritime Boulonnaise, which owned the steamer *Carly* (687/1871). His work involved organising coal shipments to Boulogne, experience on which he was to build a business empire. About 1908 Samuel and his brother Theodore set up their own business as shipbrokers and coal exporters. Two other brothers, Alfred and Gustav, were later taken into the business, and Samuel Instone and Co. Ltd. became a limited company on 3rd October 1910. Within a few years it could claim to be represented in Cardiff, London, Newcastle, Glasgow and Swansea. Samuel remained resident in Cardiff, whilst Theodore worked in London.

When war broke out in 1914 the German advance was halted only after most of the coal mining regions of northern France had been occupied. With Belgian coal also unavailable, France became heavily dependent on Great Britain for its fuel supplies. Instone quickly realised this, and is reported to have time chartered up to 40 Norwegian and Swedish steamers expressly to carry coal from British ports to France. Post-war accounts note that this venture, undoubtedly aimed at turning a profit, was a 'patriotic' one in which the earnings of these ships was 'brought into this country instead of going abroad'. To further these earnings,

S. Instone and Co. (Paris) Ltd. was set up in May 1915 to import coal to France. In addition there was also Societe Anonyme Instone in France and Compagnie Generale de Transports de Industrieele, whilst S. Instone and Co. (Italy) Ltd. had offices in London and Genoa.

## Into ship owning
For ambitious entrepreneurs like the Instones, the obvious way to extend their business was to own ships to move their coal, and in January 1915 Samuel Instone and Co. Ltd. bought the *Collivaud* from Leith owners. The 29-year-old steamer would have been no stranger to Cardiff, where she had been built and where her original owners, Morel Brothers, were based. In July 1915, a second ship, the larger and newer *Woolston*, was bought from another Cardiff owner. As will be apparent from the fleet list, Instones' ship owning began in London, mostly shifted to Cardiff towards the end of the First World War, only to revert to London in the 1930s.

In August *Collivaud* was sold and *Woolston* transferred to the Woolston Steamship Co. Ltd. This company had been incorporated in London on 5th July 1915, with a

Top: Funnel and flag of the Instone shipping companies. *[J.L. Loughran]*
Above: Acquired early in 1915, *Collivaud* was Samuel Instone's first shipping investment. She is seen in the colours of former owners, Morel Ltd. *[York Series; Roy Fenton collection]*

nominal capital of £40,000. Of this only £17,000 was ever allotted, all to the 'parent' company Samuel Instone and Co. Ltd., except for a single one pound share to each to its five directors. These worthies comprised the four Instone brothers plus a Marcus Davis, a one-time master mariner who appears in the ships' registration documents as their managing owner. With the value of ships inflating rapidly, £17,000 was quite inadequate to pay for the *Woolston*, and a mortgage for £25,000 was arranged. Over the next 18 months, Woolston Steamship was to add another four steamers, *Neilrose*, *Florence Pile* (renamed *Carly*, in memory of the first vessel with which Samuel Instone was associated, but which was soon wrecked), *Knutsford* and *Alexandra*.

In March 1918 *Carston* and *Neilrose* were sold, and two months later *Woolston* was torpedoed, becoming the only ship lost to enemy action out of the 17 owned by Instone companies at some time during the First World War. Although three further ships were acquired by Woolston Steamship, *Onwen* in 1918, *Pontwen* in 1919, and a second *Woolston* in 1920, the company had accumulated very considerable reserves from its profitable ship sales plus insurance payouts on those it lost. With over £85,000 in its reserve account in March 1920, the Instones agreed to wind up the company, with remaining vessels being sold or transferred to Samuel Instone and Co. Ltd. of Cardiff, making a significant addition to the parent company's coffers.

Samuel Instone and Co. Ltd. at Cardiff had acquired two ships of its own during the war. These included the *Arthur Balfour* which was renamed *Carston* in line with the name of *Woolston*. However, the coasters *Thordis* and *Laurium* plus the Whitby-owned *Larpool* retained their names.

## Into the red

Not all of Instones' wartime ventures were so successful financially. The Instone Transport and Trading Co. Ltd. was registered in Cardiff on 26th May 1917 with the massive nominal capital of £500,000. Its objective was to buy a fleet of coastal steamers from neutral countries to carry coal and coke from England to north French and Bay ports. To quote its prospectus, 'There is no need to enlarge upon the present difficulties which exist in the supply of coals to France for manufacturing and industrial purposes. The greater part of the French coalfields are at the present time unavailable for the purposes of supply, and although the English merchants, in conjunction with the English and French Government Authorities, have done and are doing their best to supply France with the coal required, there have been and at present are great difficulties and delays. Further hindrances have recently occurred on account of the serious shortage of tonnage and the difficulty of arranging for the chartering of steamers to carry coal. These difficulties have been accentuated by the irksome and almost impossible conditions and time charter rates demanded by neutral owners.' As an example, the total monthly cost of hiring a 1,500 ton steamer at the time is quoted as £11,250, a figure which 'is rapidly increasing'.

Samuel Instone. *[National Museums of Wales]*

The flotation was aimed squarely at Instones' existing customers in France. Only they could buy shares, and as an incentive to invest were promised that, if they subscribed up to 65% of the purchase price of a steamer, they would have the exclusive use of that ship. There was, of course, the threat of requisition of any ship by the British government, and the prospectus was at pains to point out that the British Admiralty had undertaken not to requisition neutral ships transferred to the British flag except in cases of extreme urgency, and would then pay market rates. Instones also appear to have gained the Board of Trades' agreement to import neutral ships.

The prospectus is unusually modest in its promise of quick profits, noting that the immediate benefit to subscribers would be in continuing to receive coal shipments at affordable prices. However, it was expected that, after the war, shortage of steamers would inflate the value of those bought and, with freight rates high, allow large trading profits to be made. Calculations are presented showing just how much would be earned by a fleet of ten 1,500 ton steamers running coal to Rouen.

Results fell far short of expectations. Of the £500,000 nominal capital, just under £107,000 had been subscribed by the time of the Armistice in November 1918. This came from 75 French industrialists representing a wide variety of businesses: brewing, porcelain, tanning, chemicals, laundries, paper making, printing and even corset making. It seems that few responded to the offer of having their own dedicated steamer: by far the largest investment made, £17,500 by a large dairy company, would not have bought 65% of a steamer a ruling prices. A total of £40,000 was subscribed by the founding shareholders, who were members of the Instone family, Marcus Davis and a coal importer in Paris.

Finding neutral vessels to buy proved difficult. The high freight rates that Scandinavian, Dutch and other neutral steamers could command ensured they would only be sold at vastly inflated prices. Indeed, to obtain any steamers at all, Instones had to go as far as Argentina. In Buenos Aires they first found two coasters that had been built by the respected Paisley builder John Fullerton and Co. in 1905, *Las Palmas* and *La Plata*. These were noted in register books as being for river use, and probably had to be adapted for a long ocean voyage (this would have been necessary on their delivery voyage, of course). Crews had to be recruited, and sent out to Argentina from the United Kingdom.

The two steamers left Buenos Aires on 11th August 1917, the *Las Palmas* under command of a Simon McKenzie, *La Plata* under Thomas Cavendish. Via Montevideo and Rio de Janeiro they proceeded to Pernambuco from where they set out on the long ocean passage to the Cape Verde Islands on 31st August. The two steamers lost touch with one another in the South Atlantic, with *La Plata* arriving first on 9th September and then waiting two days for *Las Palmas* to catch up. *La Plata* arrived at Bristol on 29th September, *Las Palmas* coming in on 4th October. They were quickly put to work, and by 15th October both were discharging coal in Dieppe. Names had been chosen and approved by the Board of Trade whilst they were on passage, although it took until late in November for the sisters to enter the British registry as *Plaston* and *Palmston*. Registration was in London, probably because, although nominally owned in Cardiff, they were to be managed by Instones' London office.

Unfortunately, *Plaston*, having survived her long ocean passage, worked between Cardiff, Dieppe and Rouen for barely ten weeks before being wrecked on the coast of France. After an insurance claim was paid, her accident lost the company just £342.

Not until April 1918 did there follow further vessels: three smaller, twin-screw steamers built in Germany. Again, Captains McKenzie and Cavendish were sent out to bring the two back, with a Captain Bousfield to command the third. Their routes to Europe were the same as the earlier pair, setting out from Buenos Aires individually in January 1918, taking up to two months to reach Europe. Again they were put to work before April 1918 when they were registered, this time at Cardiff, as *Newston*, *Swanston* and *Longston*.

It was expensive to buy these steamers, the four survivors having cost a shade under £150,000. But it also proved ruinous to bring them to Europe: a massive £32,000 being recorded in the company's accounts. Their voyages were protracted, as could have been predicted, but do not seen to have been unduly delayed, and it is concluded that expensive preparatory work may have been needed in Argentina. The result was a loss of over £38,000 for the first year's trading. Even with the company's four surviving ships trading for the whole of the year to June 1919, a loss of over £4,000 was recorded. No later balance sheets have survived, but the situation could not have improved, as in September 1921 the directors decided to wind up the company, and transferred the four steamers to Samuel Instone and Co. Ltd.

The price the company paid to buy and bring home its ships was clearly too high, but both were predictable for an established shipping company like Instones. Less predictable was the congestion in ports which continued after the war and which limited the company's ability to earn money. There may also have been mechanical issues with the steamers, as *Longston* went up

to the Clyde in July 1918, not returning to trade until December.

With the limited uptake by French investors, Instones and associates had invested £40,000 of their own money, and had borrowed over £81,000 by way of mortgages on their steamers. Fortunately, their ship owning and exporting activities, plus the earnings of the Woolston company, more than compensated for the losses. Although purchase of vessels such as the second *Woolston* from Sweden and the German prize *Hans Hemsoth* from the British government in early 1921 would have been expensive, the Instone fleet would have traded very profitably in the immediate post-war period.

## Into the red, again

As if the problems of the over-optimistic Instone Transport and Trading Co. Ltd. were not enough, in July 1919 a further ambitious ship owning venture was floated. The Rumney Steamship Co. Ltd. of Cardiff was to take over the five-year-old steamer *Onwen* and it was confidently predicted to earn profits of £30,000 per year and to pay a dividend of between 10 and 12.5%. Nominal capital was a massive £500,000, but the company was to commence trading when just £100,000 had been subscribed, quite insufficient to buy from the Woolston company for £180,000 the *Onwen*. Marcus Davis and one other were directors, the Instone family not being numbered among them, except for a short period in 1920 when Samuel stepped in. He and other Instones did subscribe, however, and Samuel was clearly an instigator of the venture, as the name of the company and that soon bestowed on *Onwen* reflected that of his home at Rumney Court, near Cardiff.

What is remarkable about the Rumney company is how quickly it attracted an army of small investors: over a thousand of them, with £1,000 being by far the maximum subscription from an individual. Subscribers were widely scattered geographically, and it would be interesting to know how they were recruited, although 1919 was a year of almost reckless investment in shipping companies. Samuel Instone and Co. Ltd. put in £10,000 and the Woolston company took £50,000 in shares in part payment for *Onwen*. Even so, investment reached only just over £100,000 and an £80,000 mortgage was needed on the company's steamer.

*Rumney* was put into the same trades as the other large Instone steamers, mainly running with coal out to the Mediterranean or to South America, and usually returning with grain. During the first six months of 1920, for instance, *Rumney* loaded coal on the Tyne for Trieste, calling then at Benisaf and Garrucha in Spain to load for Grangemouth. She then went round to Cardiff for another coal cargo, this time for Rosario.

Initial profits were good: almost £27,000 for 1920 and just under £26,000 for 1921. But then freight rates fell through the floor, and there was no profit in 1922 or 1923 – although balance sheets for these years have not survived. The expensively bought *Rumney* was sold in January 1924 and the company was quickly wound up, as 'by reason of its liabilities, it cannot continue'. Many small investors would lose money, as did the Instones themselves, despite what the company's prospectus claimed was their 'successful experience of running steamers'.

## Into the air

In 1909 Samuel Instone's interest in aviation led his company to sponsor an airship, proudly named *City of Cardiff*, which flew from South Wales to London and then on to France, becoming the first airship to cross the English Channel. In October 1919 this interest, along with that of his brother Alfred, who was a keen pilot, resulted in the Instone Air Line. Initially the purpose was to maintain communications with Instones' Paris business, as sending bills of lading by post could take so long that unloading of coal from steamers was unduly delayed. Aircraft operated privately from Cardiff via Hounslow Heath Aerodrome in London to Le Bourget in Paris. The London to Paris route become a public air service in April 1920 and in 1921 the business became a private limited company, taking over the aircraft plus buildings at Croydon Airport, to operate what its prospectus described delightfully as 'services of aerial conveyances'. Instone Air Line Ltd. was a private company, owned largely by the Instones themselves.

A route was opened to Cologne in May 1922, and Brussels and Prague are also reported as destinations, several of these services being given the incentive of a subsidy by the British government. However, the pioneering Paris route closed in October 1922 due

Vickers Vimy G-EASI *City of London* and a BAT FK26, probably G-EAPK, both of Instone Air Lines Ltd. *[Marvin G.Goldman (left), Barrie James (right), both courtesy William M. Demarest]*

to intense competition. An interesting claim to fame of Instone Air Line is that in January 1921 it introduced uniforms for its pilots and staff which were based on those of the merchant service, and is believed to be the first airline ever to do so. Nine different types of aircraft were operated, including a commercial version of the Vickers Vimy bomber. This would have been quite familiar to one Instone's pilots, Sir Arthur Whitten Brown, partner of Sir John Alcock in flying the Atlantic for the first time. Names of aircraft which the airline operated included *City of Cardiff*, a de Havilland DH 18, and the Vickers Vimy *City of London* (G-EASI).

During 1923 the British government decided to merge all the UK airlines into a single, more financially robust entity. Thus, Imperial Airways was formed, bringing together the services of Instone Air Line, Handley Page Transport, Daimler Airway and British Marine Air Navigation Co. Ltd. Instone Air Line ceased operations on 1st April 1924, with Sir Samuel Instone becoming a director of Imperial Airways (he had been knighted in 1921). Its assets transferred to Imperial, Instone Air Lines Ltd. was wound up in July 1924.

A present day descendant of Instone Air Lines, Instoneair offers specialist services for flying racehorses or exotic animals.

**Into the ground**
Samuel Instone sought not just to export and distribute coal, but also to profit from its mining. Indeed, coal mining became the principal business of the Instones from 1924 after the closure of the airline and the run down of their sea-going fleet. A 1921 prospectus describes Samuel Instone simply as a 'colliery proprietor'.

The first major investment was in 1918, when Samuel Instone and Co. Ltd. bought the Askern Coal and Iron Co. Ltd., owners of Askern Main Colliery, which had begun producing coal in 1912. The village of Askern, north of Doncaster, had a reputation as a spa but this did not survive the building of a colliery, brickworks and – worst of all – a coking plant. With an estimate 500,000,000 tons of coal available, Instones ambitiously predicted that the colliery would produce one million tons annually for 300 years. The previous owners had begun building houses for their workers, somewhat misleadingly dubbing these Askern Model Village. Instones continued this work, enlarging the planned houses and including bathrooms, immodestly renaming the village Instoneville. Streets named after the company's principals or ships included Instone Terrace, Alfred Street, Theodore Street, Davis Road and Airstone Road. Overcoming geological faults in the coal seams meant that it took until late 1931 for the colliery to become profitable, by when it was employing almost three

thousand men. In that year the parent company declared a profit of £7,121: fairly modest given that its capital amounted to £871,942. However, in the 1930s the government imposed a quota system to maintain the price of coal in the face of falling demand, and Askern's production was capped well below its potential output. Only during the Second World War was it restored to profitability, but even then the predicted million tons per year output was never achieved.

In 1921 Instones also bought for over half a million pounds the Bedwas Navigation Colliery at Trethomas, a few miles north of Caerphilly. It too was an important pit, employing 2,578 men in 1923 and producing half a million tons of good quality steam coal, but it too was bedevilled with geological problems. A third colliery was bought in 1924, Hoyland Silkstone Colliery near Barnsley, but was sold within a year.

Instone ownership of the two remaining collieries continued until the coal industry was nationalised in January 1947. Bedwas did not reopen

Askern Main Colliery. *[Neil Parkhouse collection]*

First and only ship built for Instones: the *Inston* of 1921. *[National Museums of Wales]*

Committee of the Board of Trade during the First World War and subsequently represented the Chamber of Shipping at the Air Conference in London in 1920 and the International Chamber of Commerce at the League of Nations.

In 1940 the *Alpheus* was joined by the ageing steam coaster *Dublin* which was renamed *Themston*, in a last hurrah for a naming scheme that had been fortuitously suggested by the first *Woolston*. By now there were no premises in Cardiff, only the London office, although the company later took an office at Bathurst Wharf, Bristol.

A new company, Instone Lines Ltd., was registered on 25th February 1944 with the very modest paid up capital of £5,002, a wholly-owned subsidiary of Samuel Instone and Co. Ltd., which itself had a much less modest paid-up capital of £256,761. Post-war expansion of the new company's fleet began first with management of two motor coasters, *Empire Seagreen* and *Empire Seablue*, for the Ministry of Shipping. These were part of a group of six wartime-built coasters that had much in common, including their ugliness, with the Empire F type developed from the CHANTs. Renamed simply *Seagreen* and *Seablue* on their acquisition by Instone, they set a naming pattern for two further acquisitions, the British-built motor coaster *Janet Plym* which became *Seahorse* in 1952 and the German war prize *Fredor* which was renamed *Seashell* in 1957. Meanwhile,

## Back into shipping

The early post-war years saw ships continue to come and go from the fleet of Samuel Instone and Co. Ltd., including its only new delivery, the *Inston*. She had been ordered during the immediate post-war boom in shipping, and her completion was somewhat protracted: launched in August 1920 she was not ready until the following January. She was sold less than two years later, amidst the run down of the fleet which saw the last of the deep-sea ships, the former German *Hans Hemsoth*, going in 1924. The four surviving ex-Argentinean coasters were transferred to this company in September 1921 but were sold in 1923, except for *Swanston* which foundered in the English Channel in December 1922. This left just the X-lighter *Airston* and the ketch *Parkend*, both acquired in 1920 and considerably smaller than the rest of the fleet. Quite possibly the former was originally bought to facilitate moving coal from smaller, less congested ports, in order to tranship it to Instone's larger ships, although *Parkend* would be of most use as a storage hulk. Sale of *Airston* in 1928 left Instones without ships but, oddly, another X-lighter, *Alpheus*, was bought in 1934 from the man to whom *Airston* had been sold, and who was now bankrupt.

Sir Samuel Instone died in 1937, leaving Theodore, Alfred and F.A. Instone as directors of the remaining Instone companies. Samuel had served on the Cardiff Executive

after the miners' strike in 1984/85, despite having the largest known coal reserves of any South Wales colliery, whilst Askern survived until 1991.

*Seagreen*, bought in 1950. *[Fotoflite incorporating Skyfotos]*

*Seablue* sank after striking a wreck off the Scheldt in 1954, the last of the company's four losses through marine hazards. The *Seashell* was sold in 1969 terminating the Instone's ship owning business.

With the Instone family's wide interests, shipping seems to have been a means to an end – albeit a profitable one – rather than an activity to which they devoted themselves wholeheartedly. With 28 ships owned over 54 years, their fleet was not insubstantial, but the ships came and went, and returned when profitable opportunities presented themselves. The variety owned, from substantial ocean-going tramps, through steam and diesel coasters, down to the tiny *Alpheus* and *Parkend*, and the rapidity with which they were bought and sold during the First World War, all these factors suggest a pragmatic approach to ship owning rather than the devotion to this business displayed by longer-lived concerns.

Instones' last ship, the Swedish-built *Seashell*, sold in 1969. *[Ships in Focus]*

# Fleet list

## 1. COLLIVAUD 1915
O.N. 89208 1,369g 872n.
240.9 x 33.1 x 18.0 feet.
C. 2-cyl. (29 and 56 x 36 inches) by Palmers' Shipbuilding and Iron Co. Ltd., Jarrow-on-Tyne; 132 NHP.
*20.3.1886:* Launched by the Bute Shipbuilding, Engineering and Dry Dock Co. Ltd., Cardiff (Yard No. 3).
*19.6.1886:* Registered in the ownership of the Collivaud Steamship Co. Ltd. (Morel Brothers and Co., managers), Cardiff as COLLIVAUD.
*1895:* Managers became Morel Ltd.
*9.11.1912:* Sold to The New Line Steamship Co. Ltd. (Richard Mackie and Co., managers), Leith.
*30.1.1915:* Acquired by Samuel Instone and Co. Ltd., London.
*12.8.1915:* Renamed BALHAM.
*18.8.1915:* Sold to the Balham Steamship Co. Ltd. (Harold Harrison, manager), London
*31.1.1917:* Owners became John Harrison Ltd., London.
*6.1.1920:* Resold to The New Line Steamship Co. Ltd. (Sir Richard Mackie and Co., managers), Leith.
*1922:* Sold to Nicola Fasano, Naples, Italy and renamed S. ANTONIO.
*1923:* Renamed FASANO.
*1925:* Sold to Barzilay ve Benjamen Vapur Kumpanyasi, Istanbul, Turkey and renamed VEFA.

*1934:* Sold to Sadikzade Nazim Kaptan, Istanbul, Turkey and renamed SUAT.
*21.5.1943:* Mined and sunk at Ereğli in the Black Sea. Salvaged, repaired and returned to service.
*1947:* Owners became Suat Sadikoglu ve Ortaklari Komandit Sirketi, Istanbul, Turkey (son of Sadikzade Nazim).
*1956:* Sold for breaking up at Istanbul-Fener, Turkey.

## 2. WOOLSTON (1) 1915-1918
O.N. 112723 2,986g 1,902n.
325.4 x 46.5 x 22.6 feet.

T. 3-cyl. (24, 40 and 65 x 42 inches) by John Dickinson and Sons Ltd., Sunderland; 292 NHP, 1,350 IHP, 9½ knots.
*6.1900:* Completed by John Blumer and Co., Sunderland (Yard No 154).
*25.6.1900:* Registered in the ownership of Claverhill Steamship Ltd. (Edmund Haslehurst and Co., managers), London as CLAVERLEY.
*21.2.1906:* Sold to Wing Steamship Co. Ltd. (Norman G. Hallett and Co., managers), Cardiff and later London.
*28.6.1906:* Renamed WHITE WINGS.
*20.1.1913:* Sold to Hants Steam Navigation

*Woolston* (1), seen as *White Wings*. *[York Series/Roy Fenton collection]*

Co. Ltd. (Harry A. Williams and Co., managers), Cardiff.
*31.3.1914:* Renamed WOOLSTON.
*1915:* Managers became Jopling and Williams, Cardiff.
*9.7.1915:* Acquired by Samuel Instone and Co. Ltd., London.
*25.8.1915:* Transferred to the Woolston Steamship Co. Ltd. (Samuel Instone and Co. Ltd., managers), London.
*14.5.1918:* Torpedoed and sunk by the German submarine UC 52 about 1.5 miles off Syracuse Harbour in position 37.30 north 012.20 east whilst outbound from Syracuse under escort of Italian trawlers bound for Messina with a cargo of sulphur. 19 of her crew were killed.
*24.5.1918:* Register closed.

### 3. NEILROSE 1915-1918
O.N. 124124  3,542g 2,243n.
335.5 x 49.7 x 24.3 feet.
T. 3-cyl. (25, 41 and 67 x 45 inches) by J.G. Kincaid and Co., Greenock; 330 NHP, 1,850 IHP, 9-10 knots.
*19.9.1905:* Launched by A. McMillan and Son Ltd., Dumbarton (Yard No. 403).
*3.1906:* Completed.
*31.7.1906:* Registered in the ownership of the Steamship Garscube Co. Ltd. (Thomas M. McCrindell, manager), Glasgow as GARSCUBE.
*18.10.1909:* Sold to David Russell, Edinburgh (Edward B. Babtie, Glasgow, manager).
*3.11.1909:* Renamed CRAIGMHOR.
*20.12.1909:* Transferred to the Craigmhor Steamship Co. Ltd. (David Russell, manager), Leith.

*23.1.1913:* Sold to the Neil Steamship Co. Ltd., London.
*4.3.1913:* Renamed NEILROSE.
*2.4.1913:* Sold by the mortgagees (J. Holman and Sons Ltd., London) to Cyril H. Walton, London.
*18.11.1913:* Sold to the Neilrose Steamship Co. Ltd. (Letricheux and David Ltd., managers), Swansea.
*28.9.1915:* Acquired by the Woolston Steamship Co. Ltd. (Samuel Instone and Co. Ltd., managers), London.
*5.3.1918:* Sold to the Charlton Steam Shipping Co. Ltd. (Charlton, McAllum and Co. Ltd., managers), Newcastle-on-Tyne.
*13.7.1918:* Renamed HEATHSIDE.
*15.8.1919:* Sold to Edward R. Care and Leonard B. Marquand, Cardiff.
*24.9.1919:* Transferred to the Care and Marquand Shipping Co. Ltd., Cardiff.
*23.2.1921:* Renamed ARNCLIFFE.
*25.11.1925:* Sold to the Britain Steamship Co. Ltd. (Watts, Watts and Co. Ltd., managers), London.
*2.1926:* Renamed COOKHAM.
*1.6.1932:* Register closed, broken up at Bilbao during the second quarter.

### 4. CARLY 1916
O.N. 101934  3,358g 2,193n.
330.5 x 43.2 x 21.6 feet.
T. 3-cyl. (24, 38 and 64 x 42 inches) by Central Marine Engine Works, West Hartlepool; 300 NHP, 1,200 IHP, 9 knots.
*25.7.1892:* Launched by William Gray and Co. Ltd., West Hartlepool (Yard No. 441).
*9.1892:* Completed.
*7.10.1892:* Registered in the ownership of the

Quantock Steam Ship Co. Ltd. (G.L. Tapscott and Co., managers), London as QUANTOCK.
*14.12.1896:* Managers became J. Holman and Sons, London.
*21.6.1897:* Sold to Charles W. Harrison, London.
*19.7.1897:* Sold to J. Weatherill and Sons, Dublin.
*24.7.1897:* Renamed FLORENCE PILE.
*1.1.1916:* Acquired by the Woolston Steamship Co. Ltd. (Samuel Instone and Co. Ltd., managers), London.
*10.1.1916:* Renamed CARLY.
*24.8.1916:* Wrecked on La Blanche Rocks about 14 miles west of St. Nazaire whilst on passage from Villaricos for Nantes with a cargo of iron ore
*26.9.1916:* Register closed.

### 5. KNUTSFORD 1916
O.N. 113124  3,842g 2,489n 6,250d.
340.0 x 47.1 x 27.1 feet.
T. 3-cyl. (25, 40 and 67 x 45 inches) by Richardsons, Westgarth and Co. Ltd., Middlesbrough; 314 NHP, 1,600 IHP, 9 knots.
*15.6.1903:* Launched by Robert Stephenson and Co. Ltd., Hebburn-on-Tyne (Yard No. 79).
*30.7.1903:* Registered in the ownership of Robert B. Stoker, Manchester as KNUTSFORD.
*8.9.1903:* Owners became Steamship Knutsford Ltd. (Robert B. Stoker, manager), Manchester
*29.12.1913:* Sold to Gripwell Steamship Co. Ltd. (Roth Brothers (London) Ltd., managers), London.
*30.12.1913:* Renamed GRIPWELL.

*Cookham*, formerly *Neilrose*, laid up. *[Roy Fenton collection]*

*Knutsford arriving at Boston, U.S.A. 7th July 1913. [R. Hildebrand/Eric Johnson]*

*5.8.1914:* Re-possessed by Steamship Knutsford Ltd. (Robert B. Stoker, manager), Manchester as mortgagees.
*21.12.1914:* Renamed KNUTSFORD.
*28.4.1916:* Sold to the Leeds Fireclay Co. Ltd. (T.H. Evans and Co., managers), London.
*26.6.1916:* Acquired by the Woolston Steamship Co. Ltd. (Samuel Instone and Co. Ltd., managers), London.
*22.7.1916:* Sunk by gunfire from the Austro-Hungarian submarine U 39 12 miles north west by north of Cape Corbelin in position 37.03 north, 04.17 east whilst on a voyage from Tunis to Baltimore with a cargo of zinc ore.
*16.8.1916:* Register closed.

### 6. CARSTON 1916-1918
O.N. 109727 3,849g 2,499n.
340.0 x 47.1 x 20.0 feet.
T. 3-cyl. (24¾, 40 and 67 x 45 inches) by Richardsons, Westgarth and Co. Ltd., Middlesbrough; 312 NHP, 1,600 IHP, 9 knots.
*27.3.1903:* Launched by Robert Stephenson and Co. Ltd., Hebburn (Yard No. 78) for the British Maritime Trust Ltd., West Hartlepool as GLORIANA but sold during fitting out.
*21.5.1903:* Registered in the ownership Robert M. Coverdale t/a John Coverdale and Son, Hartlepool as FRANK COVERDALE.
*14-23.8.1912:* Sold to the Arthur Balfour Steamship Co. Ltd. (Sanderson Brothers and Jones, managers), West Hartlepool.
*28.8.1912:* Renamed ARTHUR BALFOUR.
*31.10.1916:* Acquired by Samuel Instone and Co. Ltd., Cardiff.
*29.1.1917:* Renamed CARSTON.
*12.3.1918:* Sold to the Bathampton Steam Navigation Co. Ltd. (Christie and Co., managers), Cardiff.
*25.6.1921:* Register closed on sale to Charles D. Paschalis, Alexandria, Egypt.
*1926:* Sold to Diapoulis and Dambassis, Andros, Greece and renamed GOULANDRIS.
*6.11.1932:* Foundered about five miles south of Crete whilst on a voyage from Karavostassi, Crete to Stettin with a cargo of iron ore.

### 7. ALEXANDRA 1916-1924
O.N. 119220 3,865g 2,484n.
346.5 x 49.6 x 25.6 feet.
T. 3-cyl. (25, 41 and 67 x 45 inches) by George Clark Ltd., Sunderland; 338 NHP, 1,500 IHP, 10 knots.
*11.1905:* Completed Short Brothers Ltd., Sunderland (Yard No. 327).
*2.11.1905:* Registered in the ownership of the Taylor and Sanderson Steam Shipping Co. Ltd. (Taylor and Sanderson, managers), Sunderland as ALEXANDRA.
*16.11.1916:* Acquired by Woolston Steamship Co. Ltd. (Samuel Instone and Co. Ltd., managers), Cardiff.
*17.3.1920:* Transferred to Samuel Instone and Co. Ltd., Cardiff.
*26.5.1924:* Register closed on sale to A/S Inger (Jacob Kjode A/S, managers), Bergen, Norway and renamed INGERFIRE.
*10.4.1940:* Arrived in Tromso from the U.S.A. just after the German invasion of Norway and was used to carry coal from Svalbard.
*8.6.1940:* Whilst on passage from Svalbard for Tromso with a coal cargo, redirected to Thorshavn, Faeroes and then escaped to the UK following the capitulation of Norway.

*11.1942:* Took part in Operation Torch as an ammunition and supply ship.
*11.4.1943:* Torpedoed and sunk by the German submarine U 613 in position 51.29 north, 42.59 west whilst on ballast passage from Barrow-in-Furness to Halifax, Nova Scotia for orders. She had lost contact with convoy ONS 2 during heavy weather and was proceeding ahead of the convoy as a 'romper'. Six Norwegian and two British members of the crew died and the 28 survivors were picked up by HMCS ST CROIX and HMCS CAMROSE on 12.4.1943.

### 8. THORDIS 1917
O.N. 133569 509g 283n.
160.1 x 27.2 x 11.0 feet.
C. 2-cyl. (13 and 29 x 23 inches) by Porsgrund Mekinisk Vaerksted, Porsgrund; 52 NHP, 350 IHP, 9 knots.
*14.12.1904:* Launched by Porsgrund Mekinisk Vaerksted, Porsgrund (Yard No.41).
*2.1905:* Completed for Actieselskab Thordis (T. Thommesen and Son), Arendal, Norway as THORDIS.
*17.2.1915:* Registered in the ownership of the Thordis Shipping Co. Ltd., Bolton (Alfred E. Bowen, manager, Manchester).
*1916:* Managers became Adam Bromley and Son, Bolton.
*14.11.1916:* Sold to the Side Shipping Co. Ltd. (George A. Connell and George W. Grace, managers), Newcastle-upon-Tyne.
*19.3.1917:* Acquired by Samuel Instone and Co. Ltd., Cardiff.
*17.9.1917:* Sold to Thordis Shipping Co. Ltd. (John Slater, manager), London.
*26.10.1917:* Sold to Thomas E. Brooke (T.G. Beatley and Son), London.
*13.7.1918:* Renamed MADAME RENEE.
*10.8.1918:* Torpedoed and sunk by the German submarine UB 30 one mile north north east of Scarborough whilst on a voyage from London to the Tyne with a cargo of copper pyrites. Ten of her crew were lost.
*16.11.1918:* Register closed.

*Carston.  [National Maritime Museum P9559]*

The only pictures found of the Turkish *Sumer*, formerly *Larpool*. *[Jochen Kruesmann]*

**9. LAURIUM 1917**

O.N. 140268 582g 337n.
174.5 x 27.0 x 11.95 feet.
T. 3-cyl. (13, 21 and 34 x 27 inches)
by C. Furness Westgarth and Co. Ltd.,
Middlesbrough; 60 NHP, 350 IHP, 8.5 knots.
*12.1896:* Completed by R. Craggs and
Sons, Middlesbrough (Yard No. 127) for
A/S D/S Gerd (B.K. Bergersen, manager),
Trondheim, Norway as GERD.
*1898:* Sold to A/S D/S Gerd (Bachke & Co.,
manager), Trondheim.
*1912:* Sold to Compagnie Française des
Mines de Laurium, Piraeus, Greece and
renamed LAURIUM.
*14.3.1917:* Registered in the ownership
of John and Cecil Dixon, London as
LAURIUM.
*25.4.1917:* Acquired by Samuel Instone and
Co. Ltd., Cardiff.
*17.9.1917:* Sold to Thordis Shipping Co.
Ltd. (John Slater, manager), London.
*23.4.1918:* Mined and sunk 15 miles east
of Skegness whilst on a voyage from Hull
to Rouen with a cargo of coal. The mine
had been laid 21.4.1918 by the German
submarine UC 64.
*24.5.1918:* Register closed.

**10. LARPOOL 1917-1919 Iron**

O.N. 82664 1,288g 836n.
240.3 x 33.5 x 17.2 feet.
C. 2-cyl. (29 and 55 x 38 inches) by John
Dickinson, Sunderland; 120 NHP, 8 knots.
*8.1880:* Launched by J.L. Thompson and
Son, Sunderland (Yard No 155).
*23.9.1880:* Registered in the ownership
of John H. Barry and Co., Whitby as
LARPOOL
*1888:* Managers became Rowland and
Marwood, Whitby.
*4.6.1891:* Sold to Edwin Jenkins and Co.,
Cardiff.
*28-30.6.1917:* Acquired by Samuel Instone
and Co. Ltd., Cardiff.
*5.11.1919:* Sold to the Humber Steam
Shipping Co. Ltd. (Peter R. Bordewich and
Co., managers), Hull.
*3.8.1923:* Register closed on sale to G.N.
Pittas, Brothers and Co. (D.N. Pittas,
manager), Chios, Greece and renamed
NICOLAOS.

*28.9.1932:* Registered at Larnaca, Cyprus in
the ownership of the Pittas Union Steamship
Co. Ltd., London (D.N. Pittas, Chios,
manager).
*15.8.1935:* Register closed on sale to
Muezzinade Ahmet Behcet ve Fuat
Akbasoglu, Istanbul, Turkey for £1,600 and
renamed SUMER.
*1939:* Transferred to Ahmet Behcet
Muezzinoglu and Fuat Akbasoglu, Izmir,
Turkey.
*1950:* Registered in the sole ownership of
Fuat Akbasoglu, Istanbul.
*1959:* Sold to Emine Uzuner ve Ortaklari
(Sukru ve Yakup Uzuner, managers), Istanbul.
*1964:* Owners became Omer Sukru Aykas ve
Celal Uzuner Donatim Ortakligi, Istanbul.
*10.1967:* Demolition began at Istanbul-Fener
by Naci Cavasoglu

**11. PLASTON 1917**

O.N. 140418 423g 241n.
160.3 x 31.1 x 9.3 feet.
C. 2-cyl. (14 and 28 x 20 inches) by Ross
and Duncan, Glasgow; 40 NHP, 8 knots.
*3.10.1905:* Launched by John Fullerton and
Co., Paisley (Yard No. 188) for La Fluviale
(Antonio Carbone, manager), Buenos Aires,
Argentina as LAS PALMAS.
*21.11.1917:* Registered in the ownership
of Instone Transport and Trading Co. Ltd.,
Cardiff (Samuel Instone and Co. Ltd.,
London, managers) as PLASTON.
*18.12.1917:* Driven ashore in a gale at Percée
Point, east of Cape Barfleur, whilst on a
voyage from Rouen to Cardiff in ballast.
*31.12.1917:* Register closed.

**12. PALMSTON 1917-1923**

O.N. 140428 430g 195n.
160.0 x 31.1 x 9.1 feet.
C. 2-cyl. (15 and 32 x 22 inches) by Colin
Houston and Co., Glasgow; 59 NHP, 360
IHP, 9 knots.
*1949:* Fitted with oil engine 2SCSA 5-cyl.
made in 1944 by Fredrikshavn Jernstoberi
und Maskinfabrik A/S, Fredrikshavn,
Denmark.
*26.7.1907:* Launched by John Fullerton and
Co., Paisley (Yard No.199) for La Fluviale
(Antonio Carbone, manager), Buenos Aires,
Argentina as LA PLATA.

*8.1907:* Completed.
*30.11.1917:* Registered in the ownership
of Instone Transport and Trading Co. Ltd.,
Cardiff (Samuel Instone and Co. Ltd.,
London, managers) as PALMSTON.
*14.9.1921:* Transferred to Samuel Instone
and Co. Ltd., Cardiff.
*12.4.1923:* Sold to Invicta Coal and
Shipping Co. Ltd. (Charles E. Hallett,
manager), Sandwich, Kent.
*13.11.1925:* Register closed on sale to
Belgium.
*3.9.1926:* Registered in the ownership of
Henry Burden Junior and Co. Ltd., Poole.
*1.2.1937:* Sold to Coast Lines Ltd.,
Liverpool.
*24.5.1937:* Sold to James Mitchell and Co.
Ltd., Leith.
*31.1.1940:* Sold to Risdon Beazley Ltd.,
Southampton.
*29.7.1946:* Sold to T. and W. Colassi Ltd.
(Noel W. Purvis, manager), London.
*20.3.1947:* Register closed on sale to A/S
Rederiet 'Anholt' (R.L. Albertsen, manager),
Copenhagen, Denmark and renamed AMOS.
*1949:* Fitted with oil engine.
*1962:* Broken up at Randers during the
fourth quarter by Logstrup and Co.

**13. NEWSTON 1918-1923**

O.N. 139627 501g 232n.
145.3 x 29.8 x 11.3 feet.
Two C. 2-cyl. (each $10^{13}/16$ and $20^{1}/16$ x
15¾) by G. Seebeck A.G., Bremerhaven,
Germany driving twin screws; 26 NHP, 7.5-
8 knots.
*1932:* Two 5-cyl. oil engines by Fairbanks,
Morse and Co., Belmont, U.S.A.; 250 BHP,
10.8 knots.
*31.7.1906:* Completed by G. Seebeck A.G.,
Bremerhaven (Yard No. 236) for Santiago
Ferrando, Buenos Aires, Argentina as
FAVORITA DONA CATALINA.
*10.4.1918:* Registered in the ownership of
Instone Transport and Trading Co. Ltd.,
Cardiff (Samuel Instone and Co. Ltd.,
London, managers) as NEWSTON.
*13.9.1921:* Transferred to Samuel Instone
and Co. Ltd., Cardiff.
*9.4.1923:* Register closed on sale to Nordsee
Linie A.G., Bremen, Germany and renamed
MARIE KOTHE.

Seen approaching the port of Copenhagen in 1961/62 is *Amos*, formerly Instone's *Palmston*. At some stage after her sale to Danish buyers in 1947 the vessel was heavily rebuilt with a new funnel, accommodation and wheelhouse, even new gear was fitted on deck. A grounding led to her scrapping in 1962. *[Fredfeldt/Bent Mikkelsen archive]*

*28.6.1924:* Sold to Hermann Schütte and Co., Bremerhaven.
*15.9.1924:* Renamed MARS.
*18.12.1925:* Sold to Harold C. Sleigh, Melbourne, Australia as MARION SLEIGH.
*24.5.1932:* Sold to Alexander F. Watchlin, Auckland, New Zealand and converted to a motor vessel.
*14.6.1932:* Renamed PORT WHANGAREI.
*26.10.1934:* Sold to Charles G. White, Wellington, New Zealand.
*30.10.1942:* Sold to the Government of New Zealand, loaned to the US Navy and operated under pennant number YAG-25.
*13.8.1943:* Register closed.
*4.1944:* Returned to owners.
*21.11.1944:* Registered in the ownership of the Union Steam Ship Company of New Zealand Ltd., Wellington, New Zealand.
*24.11.1944*: Sold to Holm Shipping Co. Ltd., Wellington and renamed HOLMBURN.
*12.2.1954:* Register closed on sale to Captain Emile Savoie, Noumea and renamed JACQUES DEL MAR.
*20. 7.1954:* Wrecked on a reef at Lord Howe Island after dragging her anchor during a storm. She was on passage from Sydney, New South Wales for Noumea with general cargo.

**14. SWANSTON  1918-1922**
O.N. 139628  484g 235n.
138.8 x 29.7 x 11.4 feet.
Two C.2-cyl. (each $10^{13}/_{16}$ and $20^1/_{16}$ x 15¾) by G. Seebeck A.G., Bremerhaven, Germany driving twin screws.
*1905:* Completed G. Seebeck A.G., Bremerhaven (Yard No 223) for Santiago Ferrando, Buenos Aires, Argentina as FAVORITO SANTIAGO FERRANDO.
*15.4.1918:* Registered in the ownership of Instone Transport and Trading Co. Ltd., Cardiff (Samuel Instone and Co. Ltd., London, managers) as SWANSTON.
*13.9.1921:* Transferred to Samuel Instone and Co. Ltd., Cardiff.

*20.12.1922:* Foundered off Start Point whilst on a voyage from Antwerp to Cardiff with a cargo of sugar and generals.
*11.1.1923:* Register closed.

**15. LONGSTON  1918-1923**
O.N. 139630  548g 263n.
154.0 x 29.7 x 11.5 feet.
Two C.2-cyl. (each 11 and 20 x 15¾ inches) by G. Seebeck A.G., Bremerhaven, Germany.

*30.3.1907:* Launched by G. Seebeck A.G., Bremerhaven (Yard No 253).
*4.1907:* Completed for A. Koppel, Buenos Aires, Argentina as FAVORITA CLARA.
*8.7.1907:* Sold to Santiago Ferrando, Buenos Aires
*18.4.1918:* Registered in the ownership of Instone Transport and Trading Co. Ltd., Cardiff (Samuel Instone and Co. Ltd., London, managers) as LONGSTON.
*13.9.1921:* Transferred to Samuel Instone and Co. Ltd., Cardiff.
*27.4.1923:* Register closed.
*8.5.1923:* Sold to Nordsee Linie A.G., Bremen, Germany and renamed TILLIE GODMANN.
*28.6.1924:* Sold to Hermann Schütte, Bremerhaven.
*15.9.1924:* Renamed JUPITER.
*12.12.1925:* Sold to G.C.A. Ipland, Hamburg, Germany.
*15.5.1926:* Sold to Santiago Ferrando, Buenos Aires and renamed FAVORITA CLARA.
*1937:* Owners became Viuda de Santiago Ferrando y Hijos, Buenos Aires and renamed FAVORITA CLARA PRIMERA.
*1959:* Reported sold to Interamericana de Navegacion S.A. Buenos Aires, renamed FAVORITA and converted to a motor vessel. However, neither this sale nor the re-engining is noted in 'Lloyd's Register'.
*1962:* Deleted from 'Lloyds Register' as non-seagoing.

*Newston* as *Port Whangarei* (top) and as *Holmburn* after her sale to the Holm Shipping Co.Ltd. in 1944. *[Ian J. Farquhar collection]*

## 16. ONWEN/RUMNEY 1918-1924

O.N. 132897  4,250g 2,707n.
363.1 x 51.0 x 26.4 feet.
T.3-cyl. (26, 43 and 71 x 48 inches) by John
Readhead and Sons Ltd., South Shields; 401
NHP, 2,200 IHP, 10½ knots.
*27.11.1913:* Launched by John Readhead and
Sons Ltd., South Shields (Yard No. 438).
*24.01.1914:* Completed.
*23.1.1914:* Registered in the ownership of the
W. and C.T. Jones Steamship Co. Ltd. (W and
C.T. Jones, managers), Cardiff as ONWEN.
*10.9.1918:* Acquired by the Woolston
Steamship Co. Ltd. (Samuel Instone and Co.
Ltd., managers), London.
*15.8.1919:* Transferred to the Rumney
Steamship Co. Ltd. (Samuel Instone and Co.
Ltd., managers), Cardiff.
*9.10.1919:* Renamed RUMNEY.
*10.1.1924:* Sold to Joseph Constantine
Steamship Line Ltd., Middlesbrough.
*14.1.1924:* Renamed KINGSWOOD.
*7.5.1928:* Register closed on sale to A/B
Naxos Prince (R. Mattson, manager),
Helsinki, Finland and renamed HOGLAND.
*21.8.1941:* Torpedoed and sunk by the Free
French submarine RUBIS off Stavanger in
position 58 28 north, 06 38 east whilst on
a voyage from Norway to a German Baltic
port with a cargo of iron ore.

## 17. PONTWEN 1919-1920

O.N. 136936  4,796g 3,020n.
380.2 x 50.9 x 28.0 feet.
T. 3-cyl. (26, 42 and 70 x 48 inches) by Blair
and Co. Ltd., Stockton-on-Tees; 385 NHP,
1,900 IHP, 9 knots.
*28.4.1914:* Launched by Richardson, Duck
and Co. Ltd., Stockton-on-Tees (Yard No.
639).
*28.5.1914:* Registered in the ownership of
the W. and C.T. Jones Steamship Co. Ltd.

*Onwen,* later *Rumney* (top) and in later life, at Montevideo on 10th April 1940 in
neutrality markings, as the Finnish *Hogland.* [*National Museum of Wales; Bill
Schell*]

(W and C.T. Jones, managers), Cardiff as
PONTWEN.
*6.1914:* Completed.
*9.4.1919:* Acquired by Woolston Steamship
Co. Ltd. (Samuel Instone and Co. Ltd.,

managers), London.
*17.3.1920:* Sold to Maindy Shipping
Co. Ltd. (Jenkins, Richards and Evans,
managers), Cardiff.
*22.7.1920:* Renamed MAINDY GRANGE.

*Pontwen* as *Maindy Grange.* [*B. and A. Feilden/J. and M. Clarkson collection*]

9.12.1921: Transferred to David R. Llewellyn, St. Fagans (D.R. Llewellyn, Merrett and Price, Cardiff, managers).
28.6.1926: Management transferred to James Rattray, Cardiff.
12.8.1932: Sold to the Tramp Shipping Development Co. Ltd. (Basil M. Mavroleon, manager), London.
20.8.1932: Register closed, registered in Panama (Rethymnis and Kulukundis Ltd., Syra, Greece, managers) and renamed MOUNT PINDUS.
1935: Sold to P.M. Poutous, Piraeus, Greece and renamed MICHALIS POUTOUS.
1936: Sold to Michael M. Xylas, Syra and renamed ARIS.
12.10.1939: Shelled then torpedoed and sunk by the German submarine U 37 in position 53.28 north, 14.30 west whilst on ballast passage from Troon for Hampton Roads. She was sailing unescorted when the submarine tried to intercept her west of Ireland but she maintained her course and, although neutral, was shelled by the submarine. Her crew abandoned ship in two lifeboats after the first shell hit and the submarine finally torpedoed the ship to sink her. Two crew members died in the action but U-boat commander Hartmann towed the survivors in their lifeboats 80 miles towards safety near the Irish coast.

## 18. WOOLSTON (2) 1920-1922

O.N. 144427 198g 103n.
100.0 x 22.2 x 9.6 feet.
C.2-cyl. (9½ and 21 x 13½ inches) by Wilhelmbergs M/V, Goteborg, Sweden; 100 IHP, 8 knots.
1901: Completed by C.A. Lundahl, Goteborg, Sweden for his own account as GLADSTONE.
1906: Sold to Svenska Cement Forsaljnings Aktieb, Malmo, Sweden.
1917: Sold to Svenska-Ryska Rederi A/B (E. Sjodin, manager), Stockholm, Sweden.
5.3.1920: Registered in the ownership of Samuel Instone and Co. Ltd., Cardiff as WOOLSTON.
12.4.1923: Sold to John Stewart, Glasgow.
14.4.1923: Sold to Peter A. Smith and James Mathieson, Glasgow.
21.2.1924: Sold to Arthur Fielding, Southport, Lancashire.
22.8.1924: Foundered about 12 miles south east of Sanda Island whilst on passage from Carnlough to Ardrossan with a cargo of limestone.
12.9.1924: Register closed

## 19. AIRSTON 1920-1928

O.N. 144523 133g 97n.
106.1 x 21.0 x 7.5 feet.
1-cyl. (12⁶³/₆₄ inch) oil engine by J and C.G. Bolinders Co. Ltd., Stockholm, Sweden; 40 BHP, 50 IHP, 6-7 knots.
1933: Oil engine 3-cyl. (200 x 300 mm) by Deutz-Motoren-Gesellschaft, Koln, Germany; 110 BHP, 142 IHP, 6½ knots.
1915: Completed by William Beardmore and Co. Ltd., Dalmuir, Glasgow (Yard No. 533N) for the Admiralty, London as the X-Lighter X 169.
27.4.1920: Registered in the ownership of Samuel Instone and Co. Ltd., Cardiff as AIRSTON.
14.9.1928: Sold to Clifford Newton, London.
11.10.1933: Sold by mortgagees to J.J. Prior Ltd., Blackwall, London and re-engined.
1934: Transferred to J.J. Prior (Transport) Ltd., Blackwall.
28.2.1937: Foundered on Maplin Sands, off Clacton-on-Sea in the Thames Estuary with the loss of all four crew members.
28.5.1937: Register closed.

## 20. PARKEND 1920-1922 Wooden ketch

O.N. 67228 192g 175n.
103.1 x 24.0 x 10.5 feet.
1873: Completed by William Bayley and Sons, Ipswich (Yard No. 17) for Sully and Co. Ltd., Bridgwater as the schooner PARKEND.
1891: Re-rigged as a ketch.
30.7.1917: Sold to Vincent A. Quenet, North Shields.
10.7.1918: Sold to Theodor Shipping Co. Ltd. (Arthur Tate and Co., managers), Newcastle-upon-Tyne.
2.11.1920: Acquired by Samuel Instone and Co. Ltd., Cardiff.
7.9.1922: Sold to Ernest Screech, Plymouth.
12.9.1922: Register closed on being reduced to a hulk following sale to Fox, Sons and Company, London.

## 21. INSTON 1921-1922

O.N. 145138 1,834g 1,054n.
270.2 x 38.2 x 16.7 feet.
T. 3-cyl. (20, 33 and 54 x 36 inches) by MacColl and Pollock Ltd., Sunderland; 178 NHP, 1,250 IHP, 10¾ knots.
30.8.1920: Launched by Charles Rennoldson and Co., South Shields (Yard No 185).
24.1.1921: Registered in the ownership of Samuel Instone and Co. Ltd., Cardiff as INSTON.

*Inston as Hillglade. [Roy Fenton collection]*

*30.11.1922:* Sold to the Portrush Steamship Co. Ltd. (McNeil and Jones, managers), London.

*2.7.1923:* Renamed HILLGLADE

*28.2.1924:* Transferred to the Portland Steamship Co. Ltd. (R. McNeil and Sons, managers), London.

*15.10.1924:* Transferred to Portsmouth Steamship Co. Ltd. (McNeil and Jones, managers), London.

*25.6.1928:* Register closed on sale to Worms et Compagnie, Le Havre, France and renamed NORMANVILLE

*7.1940:* Taken over by the UK whilst lying at Plymouth.

*5.9.1940:* Registered in the ownership of the Ministry of Shipping, London (Westbourne Shipping Co. Ltd. (William E. Hinde), Cardiff, managers).

*1941:* Owners became the Ministry of War Transport, London.

*24.7.1945:* Register closed on return to her French owners.

*1951:* Sold to Armatori Riuniti Affari Maritimi, Naples, Italy and renamed ROSALBA.

*1952:* Sold to Francesco. Longobardo, Naples, Italy.

*4.1959:* Arrived at Piraeus for breaking up

## 22. HANS HEMSOTH 1921-1924
O.N. 102965  2,487g 1,573n.
300.0 x 41.1 x 18.1 feet.
T. 3-cyl. (22½, 36½ and 60 x 39 inches) by Blair and Co. Ltd., Stockton on Tees; 200 NHP. 8.5 knots.

*19.4.1894:* Launched by Joseph L. Thompson and Sons Ltd., Sunderland (Yard No 311).

*20.8.1894:* Registered in the ownership of William Tulley and Co., Hull as AMYL.

*25.3.1895:* 32/64 transferred to the Amyl Steamship Co. Ltd. (William Tulley and Co., managers), Hull. Transfer of further shares not completed until 12.4.1897.

*23.7.1900:* Sold to Continentale Rhederei A.G., Hamburg, Germany and renamed HEIMFELD

*13.12.1911:* Sold to Frachtkontor G.m.b.H., Hamburg and renamed EMIL KIRDORF.

*29.5.1914:* Sold to See und Kanal Schiffahrt Wilhelm Hemsoth A.G., Dortmund, Germany.

*10.7.1914:* Renamed HANS HEMSOTH.

*8.1914:* Seized by the United Kingdom whilst lying at Blyth.

*31.7.1915:* Registered in the ownership of the Admiralty, London (Everett and Newbigin Ltd., Newcastle-upon-Tyne, managers) as HANS HEMSOTH.

*26.5.1921:* Acquired by Samuel Instone and Co. Ltd., London.

*23.10.1924:* Register closed on sale to Antonino Giuffrida fu Carmelo, Catania, Italy and renamed ULISSE.

*1925:* Renamed ANTEO.

*7.1929:* Arrived at Bo'ness for breaking up by P. and W. McLellan and demolished during the third quarter

*Alpheus. [Roy Fenton collection]*

## 23. ALPHEUS 1934-1947
O.N. 161343  151g 88n.
*1929:* 140g 110n.
105.7 x 21.1 x 7.4 feet.
2-cyl. oil engine by William Beardmore and Co. Ltd., Dalmuir, Glasgow; 14 NHP, 50 IHP, 6 knots.
*1929:* 2-cyl. (13 x 13³/8 inches) oil engine made by Ruston and Hornsby Ltd., Lincoln in 1918; 89 BHP, 100 IHP, 7 knots.
*1938:* 2SCSA 5-cyl. (7 x 9 inches) oil engine by Crossley Brothers Ltd., Manchester; 125 NHP, 154 BHP, 6½ knots.
*1915:* Completed by William Beardmore and Co.

Ltd., Dalmuir, Glasgow (Yard No. 533H) for The Admiralty, London as the X-lighter X 163.

*23.12.1929:* Registered in the ownership of Clifford Newton, London as ALPHEUS and re-engined.

*7.2.1934:* Acquired from mortgagees by Samuel Instone and Co. Ltd., London.

*1938:* Re-engined.

*26.4.1947:* Sold to W.R. Cunis Ltd., London

*31.10.1956:* Sailed from Brightlingsea for Northfleet with a crew of two but never arrived. She is believed to have foundered as wreckage was later found in Yantlet Creek, River Thames.

*24.7.1957:* Register closed.

In 1940 Kelly's *Dublin* (above) became *Themston* (next page, top), the last steamer acquired by Instones. *[Both: World Ship Society Ltd.]*

## 24. THEMSTON 1940-1952

O.N. 117516 711g 283n.
200.0 x 29.0 x 11.3 feet.
T. 3-cyl. (15½, 29¹/₈ and 48 x 36 inches)
by Ross and Duncan, Govan; 155 NHP,
950 IHP, 11 knots.
*4.1904:* Completed by John Fullerton and
Co., Paisley (Yard No.175).
*22.4.1904:* Registered in the ownership
of Tedcastle, McCormick and Co. Ltd.
(George Tedcastle, manager), Dublin as
DUBLIN.
*5.4.1919:* Manager becomes Alfred H.
Read, Liverpool.
*8.10.1919:* Owners became Coast Lines
Ltd., Liverpool.
*30.6.1920:* Owners became the British and
Irish Steam Packet Co. Ltd., Dublin.
*27.9.1922:* Owners became Coast Lines
Ltd., Liverpool.
*11.11.1922:* Renamed CARDIGAN
COAST.
*26.9.1928:* Sold to R. and D.A. Duncan
Ltd. (William Clint, manager), Belfast.
*17.12.1928:* Renamed DUBLIN.
*7.2.1940:* Sold to Samuel Instone and Co.
Ltd. (Reginald F. Lancaster, manager),
London.
*29.3.1940:* Renamed THEMSTON.
*1948:* Owners became the Themston
Steamship Co. Ltd. (Instone Lines Ltd.,
managers), London.
*5.6.1950:* Sold to Tyson, Edgar Shipping
Ltd. (Kenneth W. Tyson, manager),
London.
*18.9.1952:* Arrived at Rosyth to be broken
up by Metal Industries (Salvage) Ltd.
*23.9.1952:* Work began.
*2.5.1953:* Register closed.

## 25. SEAGREEN 1949-1959

O.N. 169206 518g 293n.
142.5 x 27.1 x 16.0 feet.
4SCSA 6-cyl. (10 x 13 inches) oil engine by
the National Gas and Oil Engine Co. Ltd.,
Ashton-under-Lyne, Lancashire; 330 BHP.
*10.1945:* Completed by Clelands
(Successors) Ltd., Willington- Quay-on-
Tyne (Yard No. 76) for the Ministry of War
Transport (Walford Lines Ltd., managers),
London as EMPIRE SEAGREEN.
*1946:* Owners became the Ministry of
Transport, London.
*1946:* Managers became Samuel Instone
and Co. Ltd., London.
*1949:* Acquired by Instone Lines Ltd.
(Samuel Instone and Co. Ltd., managers),
London.
*1950:* Renamed SEAGREEN.
*1959:* Sold to Captain H. Harvey, Baie
St. Paul, Charlevoix, Quebec, Canada and
renamed ST. PIERRE.
*1963:* Owners became Transport Maritime
Harvey Ltee., Ste. Foy, Quebec.
*1969:* Fitted with a new engine made in
1951.
*9.5.1974:* Holed when struck the base of
a breakwater outside the Lachine Canal,
Montreal. Entered canal and capsized.
Later raised and broken up.

Two views of *Seagreen*. [Ships in Focus; J. and M. Clarkson collection]

## 26. SEABLUE 1950-1954

O.N. 169202 518g 293n.
142.5 x 27.1 x 16.0 feet.
4SCSA 6-cyl. (10 x 13 inch) oil engine by
National Gas and Oil Engineering Co. Ltd.,
Ashton-under-Lyne, Lancashire; 410 IHP,
330 BHP, 9 knots.
*8.1945:* Completed by Clelands (Successors)

Ltd., Wallsend-on-Tyne (Yard No 75).
*8.9.1945:* Registered in the ownership of the
Ministry of War Transport, London (G.T.
Gillie and Blair Ltd., Newcastle-upon-Tyne,
managers) as EMPIRE SEABLUE
*20.3.1946:* Owners became The Ministry
of Transport, London and management
transferred to Instone Lines Ltd., London.

*15.9.1950:* Acquired by Instone Lines Ltd., London.
*2.11.1950:* Renamed SEABLUE
*13.2.1954:* Struck the wreck of the steamship
EMPIRE BLESSING (7,062/1945) in fog off
Knokke, Belgium and sank in the entrance to the
River Schelde about five miles west south west
of Vlissingen. She was inbound for Antwerp
from London with a cargo of cars and generals.
Subsequently raised but declared a constructive total
loss and broken up.
*30.6.1954:* Register closed.

## 27. SEAHORSE 1952-1962

O.N. 163011 351g 182n.
130.7 x 25.1 x 8.8 feet.
Oil engine 4-cyl. (12½ x 18¼ inches) 2SCSA by
Petters Ltd., Yeovil; 47 HP.
*1.1951:* Oil engine 6-cyl. 4SCSA by MAK
Maschinenbau Kiel A.G., Kiel, West Germany; 400
BHP.
*1962:* Oil engine 6-cyl. 4SCSA by Maschinenbau
Augsburg- Nurnberg A.G., Augsburg-Nurnberg,
West Germany.
*7.3.1935:* Launched by John Lewis and Sons Ltd.,
Aberdeen (Yard No. 132) for Frederick W. Horlock,
Mistley as JOLLY DAYS.
*4.1935:* Completed.
*1935:* Owners became F.W. Horlock's Ocean
Transport Co. Ltd., Harwich.
*4.7.1940:* Sold to Imperial Chemical Industries
(Alkali Division) Ltd., Liverpool.
*11.6.1945:* Owners became Imperial Chemical
Industries Ltd., London.
*1950:* Sold to the Plym Shipping Co. Ltd.,
Plymouth.
*1.1951:* Fitted with a new engine and renamed
JANET PLYM.
*1952:* Acquired by Instone Lines Ltd., London and
renamed SEAHORSE.
*1962:* Sold to Angelos Venetsianos, Piraeus, Greece,
renamed IRENE and fitted with a new engine.
*1967:* Sold to C. Gavrill and Co., Piraeus, Greece.
Lengthened to 170.5 feet with new tonnages of
495gt
*1971:* Sold to G.K. Gavriel, P.G. Gavriel and M. Ch.
Tsouba, Piraeus, Greece and renamed PANAGIS G.
*1975:* Sold to A. Athanassopoulos, S. Loudaros,
D. Papadimitriou and S. Athanassiou, Piraeus and
renamed AGIOS IOANNIS ROUSSOS.
*1979:* Renamed GEORGIOS A.
*1980:* Sold to Naheda Shipping Co. Ltd., Limassol
and renamed NAHEDA H.
*28.2.1980:* Foundered 125 miles off the coast of
Israel during heavy weather whilst on a voyage from
Alexandria to Beirut with a cargo of potatoes.

## 28. SEASHELL 1957-1968

O.N. 180184 339g 187n.
139.6 x 26.3 x 12.5 feet.
*1952:* 423g 267n.
176.8 x 26.3 x 19.7 feet.
2SCSA 6-cyl. (250 x 420mm) oil engine by A/B
Atlas Diesel, Stockholm, Sweden; 480 BHP.
*1944:* Launched by Lidingo Nya Varv and
Verkstader A/B, Lidingo, Sweden (Yard No. 2) as
GLUCKSBURG.
*6.1944:* Completed for H.C. Horn, Hamburg,
Germany as STADT GLUCKSBURG. On delivery
she entered service under requisition by the
Kriegsmarine.

Two views of *Seablue,* the lower one dated 8th June 1952. *[FotoFlite incorporating Skyfotos; J. and M. Clarkson collection]*

*Seahorse,* the lower photo dated 22nd July 1952 when she was busy exporting cars to Europe. *Themston* on the previous page was in a similar trade. *[Ships in Focus; J. and M. Clarkson collection]*

Taken as a prize at the end of the Second World War, *Stadt Glucksburg* had been built in Sweden for German owners in 1944. She became *Seashell* in 1957. *[FotoFlite incorporating Skyfotos, BW670853]*

*5.1945:* Seized by the Allies at Hamburg and taken over by the UK.
*1945:* Registered in the ownership of the Ministry of War Transport, London and renamed EMPIRE CONDART.
*3.1946:* Owners became the Ministry of Transport, London.
*1947:* Sold to Plym Shipping Co. Ltd.,

Plymouth and renamed FREDOR
*1952:* Lengthened.
*1953:* Sold to A.E.F. Monsen, Plymouth.
*1957:* Acquired by Instone Lines Ltd., London and renamed SEASHELL.
*12.1968:* Broken up at Tamise, Belgium by Jos. Boel and Fils

**MANAGED FOR THE MINISTRY OF TRANSPORT, London**

1. **EMPIRE SEABLUE 1946-1950** (see SEABLUE No. 26)

2. **EMPIRE SEAGREEN 1946-1950** (see SEAGREEN No 25)

The managed ships *Empire Seablue* (left) photographed on 6th July 1949 and *Empire Seagreen,* un-dated, alongside the Carron Company Wharf on the Thames. *[Both: World Ship Society Ltd.]*

**A note on nomenclature**

The acquisition of *Woolston* in July 1915 inspired a naming scheme that also reflected Instone's adopted family name. *Woolston*, a name which was repeated, undoubtedly came from the suburb of Southampton, given the title of her previous owner, the Hants Steam Navigation Co. Ltd. Of the other names in the series, all but one seem to have been made up, with the inspiration for Inston being obvious. The exception was *Swanston*, an area to the south of Edinburgh, but as Instones had little or no connection with Edinburgh, this might have been accidental.

# BELGIA/EMPIRE BELL OF 1930
## Bob Todd

*Belgia* with her original Swedish owner, probably in the Scheldt. *[Roy Fenton collection]*

In 1929 the Swedish ship owning company Förnyade Ångfartygs Aktiebolag Götha ordered a passenger/cargo ship from Nya Varvsaktiebolaget Öresund at Landskrona. As yard number 28 she was launched on 11th January 1930 and named *Belgia*. She was completed on 7th May 1930 and was managed by F. Sternhagen.

Her details as completed (and as re-registered in 1942) were as follows:
O.N. 7636  (168654)
2,023g  1,074n  (1,743.76g  921n)
286.5 x 40.2 x 16.7 feet
C. 4-cyl. (2 x16 $^9/_{16}$ inches and 2 x 35$^7/_{16}$ inches) Lentz-type by Lindholmen, Motala, Göteborg, Sweden; 124NHP.

The *Belgia* was a single deck ship with a shelter deck and raised forecastle, single funnel, two masts, straight stem, elliptical stern and five watertight bulkheads. She entered a regular service between Gothenburg and Antwerp, also calling at Flushing. Her last departure from Gothenburg was on 26th August 1939 and her voyage record card, held in the Lloyd's Collection at the Guildhall Library in Aldermanbury, London, shows her leaving Antwerp on 1st September 1939 bound for Gothenburg. There is no record of an arrival or subsequent departure from Gothenburg. The next entry on the card has her arriving at Flushing on 7th February 1940 and this is confirmed by 'Lloyd's Shipping Index'. By this point she was cargo-only and up to the beginning of June 1940 she voyaged to Rouen, Antwerp, Bergen, Methil, Bergen, Methil, Shields, Rouen and Falmouth. For the rest of the year she operated between various west coast ports of Great Britain and Gibraltar, Huelva and Lisbon.

On the 30th December 1940 she steamed from Oban northabout to Methil and London, arriving on 11th January 1941. She then went in ballast to Sunderland, loaded a full cargo of coal and set sail for London. After discharge she sailed for Sunderland in ballast but on 26th January while steaming near the Sunk Light off the Essex coast she was hit by bombs from a German aircraft and set on fire. During the night the Harwich-based escort destroyer HMS *Cotswold* arrived on the scene and, despite the darkness, the swell, the smoke and flames her captain, Lieutenant-Commander Peter John Knowling RN, carefully positioned the bow of his ship against the stern of the *Belgia* and First Lieutenant Dickens and two ratings boarded the crippled ship. Having assessed the situation they succeeded in transferring the *Belgia's* crew to the *Cotswold*. Six crew men of the *Belgia* were dead or missing. The three Royal Navy men were able to connect a towline and the fiercely burning ship was towed to Frinton and beached within sight of Walton Pier at about 12.30 on the morning of the 27th. The Royal National Lifeboat Institution's Walton lifeboat, the *E.M.E.D.* (1928) came alongside later in the day bringing out a salvage party from Harwich equipped with pumps and hoses. After a three-hour battle they managed to quell the fire and eventually extinguish it completely after another two hours.

A noteworthy report of this situation comes from a Lloyd's salvage officer in 'Lloyd's Shipping Index' of 29th January, 1941: 'London Jan. 27th: Steamer *Belgia* is ashore in 8 feet of water L.W.S.T. head on to the beach on clay bottom. Vessel is completely burnt out with exception of No. 4 hold and crew's after quarters. Fire was sufficiently under control to allow anchors to be laid out at 3 pm. Local fire brigade continuing operations to completely extinguish fire. Engine room is full of water. No survey possible until fire extinguished.'

On the 30th January the naval rescue tug *St. Mellons* (1918) and the requisitioned rescue tug *Kenia* (1927), assisted by the lifeboat *E.M.E.D.*, attempted to refloat the *Belgia* without success. The freighter was partially pumped out and on the 14th February the two tugs were successful and towed the burnt out hulk into Harwich harbour and up to Bloody Point, Shotley, where they beached and anchored her. Over the next ten weeks

*Belgia* beached on Bloody Point, Shotley, in Harwich harbour in the latter part of February 1941. Taken by Lieutenant Manners RN of the escort destroyer HMS *Eglinton* (1939). *[National Maritime Museum PM1013/2]*

her leaks were patched and temporary repairs were undertaken. After pumping out she was refloated on the 29th April and moved to a new anchorage in the River Stour.

The laid-up hulk was purchased by the Ministry of War Transport and on the 19th August 1941 left Harwich in tow for the River Tyne, arriving on the 21st August. There she underwent full repairs and refurbishment and was renamed *Empire Bell*, as reported in 'Lloyd's Shipping Index' on 18th October 1941. Her repairs were completed in April 1942 and she was re-registered in South Shields with the official number 168654, owned by His Majesty as represented by the Minister of War Transport, London. She was put under the management of James Westoll Ltd. of Sunderland, given the signal letters BDSW, and George Charles May became her master.

The *Empire Bell* sailed from the Tyne on the 24th April 1942 with coal for London and returned to the Tyne on the 4th May before going northabout to Belfast and Cardiff. Here she loaded a cargo of coal and on the 29th May she left Cardiff for Reykjavik, Iceland, arriving on the 9th June. She returned to Hull via Loch Ewe and Methil in July and then loaded coal on the Tyne for another round trip to Reykjavik, arriving back at Hull on the 1st September. Her next voyage was to be her last. After loading on the Tyne she sailed for Reykjavik on the 13th September via Methil Roads and Loch Ewe. She left Loch Ewe in a small convoy on the 22nd September and when west south west of the Faroes in position 62.19 north, 15.27 west on the 25th September 1942, she was torpedoed and sunk by the German submarine *U 442* (1942), commanded by Korvetten-Kapitan Hans-Joachim Hesse. She sank in just four minutes and ten of her crew perished.

With thanks to David Hodge for research.

## SOURCES AND ACKNOWLEDGEMENTS

We thank all who gave permission for their photographs to be used, and for help in finding photographs we are grateful to Tony Smith, Jim McFaul and David Whiteside of the World Ship Photo Library; to Ian Farquhar, F.W. Hawks, Peter Newall, Russell Priest, William Schell; and to David Hodge and Bob Todd of the National Maritime Museum, and other museums and institutions listed.

Research sources have included the Registers of William Schell and Tony Starke, 'Lloyd's Register', 'Lloyd's Confidential Index', 'Lloyd's Shipping Index', 'Lloyd's War Losses', 'Mercantile Navy Lists', 'Marine News', 'Sea Breezes' and 'Shipbuilding and Shipping Record'. Use of the facilities of the World Ship Society, the Guildhall Library, the National Archives and Lloyd's Register of Shipping is gratefully acknowledged. Particular thanks also to Heather Fenton for editorial and indexing work, and to Marion Clarkson for accountancy services.

**South West Scenes**
'Par - Coaster Port' by Jonathan Varcoe in 'Ships Monthly' for July 1991 gave background information.

**Instone**
'Cardiff Shipowners' (National Museum of Wales, Cardiff, 1986) by J. Geraint Jenkins and David Jenkins provided a useful introduction to the Instones' activities, and Dr David Jenkins kindly read and commented on a draft of the article. A Syren and Shipping publication simply

entitled 'Cardiff 1921', also provided background. Files relating to wound-up companies in the National Archives, Kew were consulted on the Woolston Steamship Co. Ltd. (BT3122901/140899), the Instone Transport and Trading Co. Ltd. (BT31/23709/147524), the Rumney Steamship Co. Ltd. (BT31/24797/156806), S. Instone and Co. (Paris) Ltd. (BT31/22819/140220) and Instone Air Lines Ltd. (BT31/26999/178336). Dave Fordham's 'Askern Main Colliery & Instoneville' (Fedj-el-Adoum, 2009) helped research Instones' colliery ownership. Wikipedia was consulted about the airline and Bedwas Colliery.

**Bank Line: the Final Years**
Particular thanks to Alistair McNab, formerly of Bank Line in Houston. Other informants were Frank Anderson, Mark Bamford of Tamahine Shipping, Charlotte Bleasdale, Paul Boot, Donald Hawkes and Nick Trott.

**Merchant Ships at Coronel and After**
Sources for Andrew Bell's article in 'Record' 59 were 'The Main Line Fleet of Burns Philp' (1980) by Wilkinson and Wilson; 'Naval Operations volume 1 History of the Great War based on Official Documents (1920) by Sir J.S. Corlett; 'The Drama of the Graf Spee and the Battle of the River Plate' (1964) by Sir Eugene Millington Drake (British Ambassador in Montevideo in 1914). Thanks also to Robin Pitaluga, sheep station owner in East Falkland.

**60/1**

This Barnard and Straker photograph was recently acquired by one of the editors, but has caused him some head scratching. It clearly depicts a *Phoenix*, but which one? The first possibility is a *Phoenix* (1,150/1883) built at Sunderland in 1883, and owned variously in London until 1897. However, more likely is *Phoenix* (3,576/1905) built by Earle's of Hull, close to where she was photographed and owned by the Phoenix Steamship Co. Ltd., managed by Hoyland and Co. also of Hull. However, she looks a typical short-sea trader, and too small for a tonnage of 3,576. Of interest are her enormouly tall topmasts, presumably there to raise a radio aerial well above the sea. Readers are invited to suggest which *Phoenix* is depicted.

**59/1 and 59/2**

Bob Todd suspects that this sunken vessel is the French passenger liner *La Champagne* (6,726/1886), being the only two-funnelled ship he knows of that was sunk in harbour during the First World War and that looks anything like the mystery ship. She was built in 1885-1886 as a four-masted, short-funnelled liner for the Compagnie Generale Transatlantique but in 1896 she was converted to quadruple expansion engines, given new boilers, her funnels were increased in height and she was reduced to two masts. On 28th May 1915 while entering St Nazaire from Colon she went aground and the next day she broke her back. The wreck was eventually broken up *in situ*.

The accompanying scan of a commercial postcard shows her wreck soon after breaking her back. On the reverse of the card is a hand written note which reads 'This ship was proceeding to St Nazaire in front of us. She struck a rock and has become a total wreck, while we passed her by within a few yards.'

### Nikobar and Abergeldie

In response to our appeal for information about the *Nikobar* and *Abergeldie* in 'Record 58', contributor Peter Myers found a detailed report about the *Abergeldie*'s belated salvage award in 'The Aberdeen Daily Journal' for 22nd January 1908, and summarised it as follows.

On 21st January, Mr Justice Bargrave Deane, at the Admiralty Division of the High Court of Justice in London, ruled in favour of a salvage award for the *Abergeldie*'s owners, the Adam Steamship Co. Ltd., Aberdeen, her master, Captain Keith, and her crew after it had been contested by the East Asiatic Co., Copenhagen, which owned the *Nikobar*, and her master, Captain Rambush.

In giving his judgment, the judge said salvage services had undoubtedly been rendered by the *Abergeldie* to the *Nikobar* and 'the only difficult question which had troubled the court was the proper amount to award by way of salvage and the apportionment of that amount'.

On 9th December 1906, the *Abergeldie*, which was on a voyage to the East, went to the assistance of the *Nikobar*, which was on fire while in the Gulf of Aden. The Danish ship's crew had left in the ship's boats and it was unclear to the court as to whether they had abandoned her or had temporarily left her before reboarding later to try and put out the fire.

The fire on the *Nikobar*, which was carrying copra and also coconut oil in casks, was in the forward holds and coal in her bunkers was also burning. Her crew left the ship at 3.30pm on the 9th, but the court was told that they had left the hatches open, while the ventilators were turned to windward so that the draught could get into the holds. A sea-cock in number 2 hold had also been left open. The court concluded that the master and crew had abandoned ship because they had done all that was possible to save the ship but their own lives were now at risk.

The *Nikobar*'s crew were picked up by the *Abergeldie*, whose master sent his chief officer, bosun, carpenter and six ABs to the Danish ship to forestall any salvage attempt by an Austrian steamer which approached the *Nikobar* at 10pm. The party from the *Abergeldie* extinguished the fire on the deck and drenched the bunker coal, so preventing the fire spreading to the rest of the ship. They also secured a towing hawser from the *Abergeldie* to the *Nikobar*, which was towed for about 25 miles before the hawser snapped. The Danish ship's crew returned to their ship and she got under way for Aden, being escorted part of the way by the *Abergeldie*.

It was also mentioned in court that a dhow, possibly manned by Arab pirates, had approached the disabled *Nikobar* and it was agreed by experts in the court that the *Abergeldie*'s presence would have deterred any attempts by pirates to seize the Danish ship.

The judge believed that Captain Rambush had done his utmost to save his ship, 'and it was only when he found that he was being deserted by his crew that he eventually thought it was no use perservering further'.

Out of the total salvage award of £8,000, the Adam Steamship Co. Ltd. was awarded £5,500, Captain Keith received £550, the chief officer £450 and the bosun £100. The remaining £1,400 was divided among the rest of the crew with the members of the salvage party receiving double the amount given to the others.

The Adam Steamship Co. Ltd. sold the *Abergeldie*, which it had employed in worldwide tramping, in 1913 to Goshi Kaisha Tatsuma Goshi, Japan, which renamed her *Gishun Maru*. On 30th January 1917 she sailed from Seattle to Yokohama with a cargo of steel and disappeared.

Another Adam cargo steamer, the *Asloun* (2,845/1890), earned her owners a salvage award of £16,500 after her epic rescue of the New Zealand Shipping Co.'s cargo steamer *Waikato* (4,767/1892) in 1899. The *Waikato*'s tail shaft had broken on 8th June 1899 when she was about 180 miles south of Cape Agulhas. She drifted powerless for 14 weeks before she was picked up in mid-September by the *Asloun*, which towed the *Waikato* to Fremantle, arriving there on 9th October, four months after becoming disabled.

**60/3.** Can anyone name this vessel? The only information from the back of the photo is that it was taken by H. Jenkins Limited, photographers of Lowestoft. Looking at the lifeboat it looks more like an Admiralty design than those usually carried by merchant ships, Also is she going out for trials - note the dress of the men on deck? *[J. and M. Clarkson collection]*

Letters, additions, amendments and photographs relating to features in any issues of 'Record' are welcomed (this month letters refer to issues 25 and 38). Letters may be lightly edited. Note that comments on multi-part articles are consolidated and included in the issue of 'Record' following the final part. Senders of e-mails are asked to provide their postal address.

**Fowey follow-ups**
I was interested in the 'Powered Coasters of Fowey' in part because of the earlier history of *Poldhu/Roselyne*. From this comes a tiny quibble. Although in the history of W.N. Lindsay it is suggested that *Roselyne* changed from *Poldhu* shortly before being sold to W.N. Lindsay, in the Fowey Powered Coasters article it suggest again that the name was changed on being sold. Not so: in fact, the first article on her in the Lindsay fleet was nearer correct. I know that we acquired her already called *Roselyne* and this was what in fact led to the suffix 'Rose' being taken over and used for our subsequent ships. It would be interesting to know when and why the name change took place. Do you suppose there is any chance of finding out?
DOUGLAS LINDSAY, 3 Rectory Court, Old Banwell Road, Locking, Weston-super-Mare BS24 8BS

I have just finished reading the latest 'Record' and most thoroughly enjoyed 'Fowey's Powered Coasters'.

Toyne, Carter and Co. Ltd. did, however, directly own at least two other steamers ( although not coasters).

On the 30th September 1946 they bought the steam tug *Gallant* from the liquidators of the Fowey Tug and Salvage Co. Ltd. and early in 1947 the steam tug *Fighting Cock* from the Liverpool Screw Towing and Lighterage Co. Ltd., which they renamed *Trethosa*. This was to enable a towage service to be continued at Fowey following the demise of the said Fowey Tug and Salvage Company Ltd.

During the early part of 1947, a new company, the Fowey Tug Co. Ltd. was formed, the main shareholders being Toyne, Carter and Co. Ltd. and Hannan, Samuel and Co. Ltd., the directors being John Louis Toyne and Sydney James Samuel and on the 2nd May 1947 the *Gallant* was transferred to the new company, and I assume that the *Trethosa* would be transferred at the same time ( I have a transcript of the *Gallant*'s registration papers but not the *Trethosa*'s).

On the 30th April 1947 two mortgages were registered against the tug *Gallant*, one for £3,500 provided by Toyne Carter and Co. Ltd. of Albert Quay, Fowey, and one for £1,500 provided by John Louis Toyne of Castledore, Par. Both mortgages were discharged on the 3rd May 1951 and on the 9th May the *Gallant* was sold to Fowey Harbour Commissioners.

The Fowey Tug Co. Ltd. continued to own and operate the tugs, and bought other tugs, until 1960 when the tugs were taken over by the Harbour Commissioners, and this probably really did end T. C. and Co.'s shipping ownership! Details and photographs of both tugs have appeared in 'Record' in the past in various articles I have submitted.
STEPHEN CARTER, Clovenstones Cottage, Baldrine, Isle of Man IM4 6D

*Gallant appeared in 'Record' 8 on page 205 and 'Record' 31, page 137, whilst* Trethosa *was featured on page 139 of 'Record' 31, and as* Fighting Cock *on page 248 of 'Record' 4. Ed.*

Ian Rae's article ('Record' 59) partially answered one question that I've long harboured. How did the name of Wigham Richardson come to be associated with the management of the ships of certain small Greek shipowners? Perhaps he'll be able to explain more about that enterprise at a later date ?

Roy's account of the misadventures of Fowey shipowners naturally caught my main attention. How on earth those managers considered that coasting in West Africa was a sensible commercial proposition defies understanding. Elder Dempster were abandoning the use of small feeder vessels by 1950 and the whole of West Africa has never had much demand for coastal vessels.

You only have to look at the atlas to see that the idea of entrepôt trade is not supported. Lagos could never have been an interchange in the manner of, say, Singapore. The Elder Dempster coasters did bring export cargoes from some places in the Niger Delta such as Abonema where the channel could not take the larger post-war ships. They also provided a service using two new colliers to convey coal for Ghana Railways from Port Harcourt to Takoradi but that trade, although it also allowed newly promoted masters to commence their careers on handier vessels, was finished by 1960. I saw one of those ships, the *Benin*, in 1964 in Lagos when, under the Greek flag, she was bringing coal to the Lagos power station whilst the government collier was out of service. Although substantially larger than the *Polperro* (2), she shared something of a likeness. Her bridge house was further forward but she did have davits and boats on the masthouse and also the same arrangement further aft. West Africa was ocean ship country. Exports (and imports) travelled to and from the interior on railways that ran north and south. Mammy lorries might run along the beach between some countries but telegrams between close neighbours had to be routed via London or Paris, according to which was the former colonial power. Farrell Lines had a single coaster that ran between Monrovia, Lower Buchanan and Cape Palmas on the Liberian coastline and of course a few coaster size ships did find their way up both the Gambia and Casamance rivers to load groundnuts in season. One small ship ran between Dakar and St.Louis up the River Senegal and a small decrepit ferry ran out of Dakar to places in Senegal southwards of the Gambia. Other than that, this was no place to earn a living as a conventional coaster.
JOHN GOBLE, 55 Shanklin Road, Southampton SO15 7RG

The thoroughly researched detail in Roy Fenton's 'Fowey's Powered Coasters' answers many questions that I have long pondered. Until a large property development obliterated it in the 1990s a modest office building overlooking Penryn's Quay on an arm of Falmouth Harbour bore 'Hannan, Samuel & Co. Ltd.' on its windows.

As a one time employee of Elder Dempster (1957-1974) I have some knowledge of the company's 'Branch Vessels' management – the Lagos, Nigeria-based coasters that, amongst much else, were feeder cargo ships for the mainline deep-sea ships plying to the UK, northern Europe and the USA. When Messrs Hannan and Samuel with their Polpen Shipping Co. subsidiary were trying to break into the Nigerian coastal shipping trades (1948-1955) concurrently, at that time Elder Dempster never had less than five ships 'on the Coast'. Three of these were C type standard design steam engined coasters designed for service in the Far East mainly built in 1945, each with a 974grt and a 1,200 dwt: they were the *Forcados* (3) 1946-62, S*apele* (3) 1946-62, and *Warri* (2) 1946-56 : two US built 'Sea-Jeeps', *Benu* (2) and *Bida* (3), which were replaced by the purpose UK-built *Baro* (2) (1,517g/1950-61) and *Benin* (4) 2,483g/1950-61).

Besides the 'Shallow-Deep Service' - tropical produce shipped out of the Niger delta's ports - Elder Dempster usually held part or all of the government contract to carry coal mined at Enugu, shipped from Port Harcourt to Lagos, to fuel Nigerian Railway's steam locos. Under John H. Joyce, Elder Dempster's highly effective managing director between 1944 and 1964, a belligerent attitude was taken to outsiders. At Wilmot Point, Lagos, the company had its own dockyard and, at all the ports called at, its own branch offices. The coasters' spares, supplies and staff arrived in Lagos on the fortnightly mailboat sailings from Liverpool. All this was probably buttressed by the company's Nigeria Manager being an ex-officio member of colonial Nigeria's executive council. Messrs Hannan and Samuel never had a chance.
ANDREW BELL, 'Gartul', Porthleven, Helston, Cornwall TR13 9JJ

*Sapele* (3) was one of three war-built steam coasters acquired by Elder Dempster in 1946, having been completed at Blyth the previous year as *Empire Pavilion*. On sale in 1962 she became the Pakistani *Mahia*, then *Safina-e-Ahmar* until broken up near Karachi in 1973. *[Ships in Focus]*

*Bida* (3) (above, probably in Liverpool) was built on the Great Lakes in 1943 as *John W. Arey* for bareboat charter to the U.K. Elder Dempster bought her in 1951, but sold her just a year later. Further names were *Basra* (Norwegian flag), *Pleias* and *Atlantic Contractor* (Greek), and *Timber Coast* (Philippines). She foundered during January 1971 in heavy weather whilst working in the Philippines.*[Tom Rayner/J. and M. Clarkson]*

The steamer *Benin* (4) (above, at Cape Town) was completed for Elder Dempster at Port Glasgow in 1950. 1960 saw her return to the U.K. where, following lay-up in Birkenhead alongside running mate *Baro* (2), she was sold to Constantines of Middlesbrough as *Yorkwood*. Further names carried from 1964, this time under the Greek flag, were *Noufaro* and *Agia Irene*. She foundered in heavy weather in Corunna Roads on 23rd July 1969 whilst on a voyage from Huelva to Ghent with a cargo of pyrites. *[Ships in Focus]*

# INDEX TO RECORD 57 TO 60
## Issue numbers are shown in bold

**Index of ships:** All ships' names in the text are listed, including proposed or other names not actually used, which are shown in brackets. Wherever possible, dates of build or other information are given to identify merchant ships. Ships listed in photo offers are not indexed.

Empire Fir (1941) **60**:236
Empire Gala (1946) **57**:15-6
Empire Glencoe (1941-48) **58**:79-80
Empire Gower (1946) **59**:149
Empire Granite (1941) **57**:50
Empire Islander (1944) **58**:79
Empire Kestrel (1919)**58**:118
Empire Leech (1929) **59**:168,172-3
Empire Mallory (1941) **58**:78
Empire Newfoundland (1943) **58**:79
Empire Nigel (1920) **60**:205
Empire Pavillion (1945) **60**:258
Empire Punch (1942) **59**:168,172
Empire Rawlinson (1944) **57**:15-6
Empire Raymond (1946) (tug) **59**:181
Empire Seablue (1945) **60**:241,250,252
Empire Seagreen (1945) **60**:241,250,252
Empire Tana (1923) **58**:81
Empros (1977) **58**:104
Encicia (1951) **57**:16
Energy (1988) **58**:94
Enfield (1862) (schooner) **57**:49
Eridan **57**:17
Erika Fritzen (1929) **57**:53
Ermioni (1902) **59**:166
Ermoupolis (1906) **57**:28
Ernest Legouvé **57**:48
Ernest Reyer **57**:48
Ernesto Che Guevara (1988/9) **58**:94
Errington Court (1909) **59**:135
Ertshandel (1907) **57**:27
Escaut (1929) **59**:168,172
Esito (1943) **58**:70
Espérance (1923) **57**:13
Essayons (1956) **57**:21-2
Essonite (1921) **57**:49
Etal (1933) **60**:196
Ethel C (1943) **59**:148
Etna (1921) **58**:73
Etoile du Sud (French trawler) **60**:208
Etrema (1936) **59**:186
Ettrickbank (1977) **60**:220-1,227
Euphrate (1955) **57**:19-21;**58**:119
Evaki (1956) **60**:231
Evangeline (2) (1891) **57**:25
Ever Lucky (1946) **57**:16
Exeter (1947) **60**:210

Fabric 18 (1944) **57**:9
Fager (1916) **57**:54
Fair Head (1906) **57**:43
Fairfree (1944) **57**:51;**58**:125-6
Fairport (1896) **59**:135
Fairtry II (1959) **60**:234
Falaise (1947) **59**:142
Falger (1916) **57**:54
Far East (1982) **58**:105
Faraday (1891) **57**:62
Farndale (1933) **60**:196
Fasano (1886) **60**:242

Fatina (1917) **57**:45
Fauvette (1935) **57**:4
Favorita (1907) **60**:246
Favorita Clara (1907) **60**:246
Favorita Clara Primera (1907) **60**:246
Favorita Dona Catalina (1906) **60**:245
Favorito Santiago Ferrando (1905) **60**:246
Fawzia (1964) **58**:99
Federica (1977) **60**:217
Felicity (HMS) (1944) **58**:126
Felix Roussel **57**:17
Ferdinand de Lesseps **58**:98
Ferreira (1869) **57**:30
Ficus **57**:50
Fidel (ex Peony Islands) **58**:91
Fighting Cock (1884) (tug) **60**:257
Findon (1957) **59**:152
Fingal (1964) **60**:222
Fionashell (1892) **57**:50
Fir (wherry) **57**:10
Firbank (1976) **60**:213,227
Firmity (1944) **59**:168,173
Fixity (1966) **60**:199
Fleetwood (sloop) **57**:43
Flevomeer (1902) **59**:166
Florence Pile (1892) **60**:238,243
Fluor (1925) **57**:49
Folkestone (1903) **59**:136,141-2
Forcados (3) **60**:258
Forest Dale (1898) **57**:28
Forst (1918) **58**:127
Fort Matanzas (1944) **59**:186
Fort Moose (1943) **58**:87
Fort Norway (1943) **58**:70
Fort Raleigh (1945) **59**:188
Fort Snelling (USS) **57**:7
Fort Spokane (1943) **58**:70
Forthbank (1973) **60**:220,227
Fortress 7 (1982) **58**:105
Fortune Sea (1979) **58**:107
Forum Express (1960) **58**:95
Foudroyant (HMS) (1798) **57**:59
Foy (1902) **59**:162-3,166
Foylebank (1983) **60**:218-9,227
Frank Coverdale (1903) **60**:244
Frank Jamieson (1956) (tug) **60**:236
Fratton (1925) **59**:138-9;**60**:200-2,205
Fratton (HMS) **60**:205
Fredor (1944) **60**:241,252
Friargate (1946) **57**:3,6
Frimar (1966) **58**:92
Frimaro (1966) **58**:92
Frisian Express (1957) **60**:195
Frotadurban (1980) **58**:109
Frotasingapore (1982) **58**:109
Frubel Clementina (1950) **58**:86
Fryken (1938) **58**:71
Fu Sheng 82 (1983) **58**:107
Funing (1978) **58**:104
Future Hope (1979) **58**:104
Fylrix (1962) **60**:195

Gabriele (1956) **57**:21
Gallant (1884) (tug) **58**:123;**60**:257
Gallieni **57**:17
Gange (1953) **57**:19-20
Garnet (lighter) **57**:10
Garonne **59**:185
Garscube (1906) **60**:243
Gasfire (1935) **59**:146,148
Gayarre (1920) **57**:57
Gazellebank (1983) **60**:227
Geddington Court (1936) **58**:71
Geier (SMS) **59**:131
Général de Sonis **57**:48
Général Faidherbe (1901) **57**:48
Geneva (1956) **57**:21
Gensteam (steam tug) (1924) **57**:10
George Borthwick (1917) (trawler) **59**:176
George Burton (1917) (trawler) **59**:177
George Livesey (1929) (tug) **57**:58
George R. Wood (1) (1919) (trawler) **59**:178
George R. Wood (2) (1960) **59**:179,183-4
George W. Campbell (1943) **57**:14
Georgios (1958) **57**:21
Georgios A (1935) **60**:251
Georgios Kontos (1946) **57**:6
Gerd (1896) **60**:245
Gerona (1927) **57**:36-7
Gertie (1902) **60**:207
Gift (1870) (barque) **57**:49
Gilmar (1960) (trawler) **59**:181
Giorita (1988/9) **58**:94
Giovanni Agneli (1956) **60**:231
Gishun Maru (1898) **60**:256
Giulia (1946) **59**:150
Giuseppe G (1898) **57**:28
Gladstone (1901) **60**:248
Glasgow (HMS) **59**:132-5
Glaucus (1921) **58**:72
Glaucus (5) (1943) **57**:33
Glenapp (1918) **58**:66
Gleniffer (1913) **57**:41
Glenogil (trawler) **59**:176
Glenstruan (1958) (trawler) **59**:180
Global Mariner (1979) **60**:215,222,227
Globe Trader (1980) **58**:103-4
Gloriana (1903) **60**:244
Gloriana (1905) **57**:25
Glorious (HMS) **57**:44
Glory (1983) **58**:108
Glory II (1941) **58**:68
Glucksburg (1944) **60**:251
Gneisenau (SMS) **59**:131,134
Gobeo (1921) **57**:37
Godavery (1955) **57**:21
Golden Gate (1980) **60**:211,227
Golden Light (1980) **58**:104
Goldmouth (1927) **57**:34
Golfo de Guanahacabibes (1977/8) **58**:92
Gonzales Lines (1962) **58**:87
Good Faith (1979) **58**:104
Good Hope (HMS) **59**:132

Goodwood (1937) **59**:144,148
Googi (1953) **60**:222
Gothia (1941) **58**:68
Goulandris (1903) **60**:244
Grafton (HMS) **57**:38
Grampian Fortune **59**:183
Grand Abeto (1950) **57**:18
Grand Faith (1980) **58**:104
Granma (yacht) **58**:83
Granton Falcon (trawler) **59**:181
Granton Kestrel (1957) (trawler) **59**:181
Granuaile (1895) **59**:140
Great Britain (1876) **57**:59
Great Eastern **59**:154
Greenfinch (1940) **57**:8
Greenheart (lighter) **57**:10
Greensea (1920) **57**:44
Gregos (1977) **60**:221
Grindon Hall (1908) **57**:55
Gripfast (1941) **59**:149
Gripwell (1903) **60**:243
Grosserman (1988/9) **58**:94
Grunda (1934) **60**:198
Gulf Venture (1950) **60**:231
Gutterman (1988) **58**:94
Gwalia (1905) **57**:64

H.P. Lenaghan (tug) **58**:82
Habana (1960) **58**:83
Hai Ji Shun (1978) **58**:105
Halia (1958) **59**:186
Haligonian Prince (1943) **58**:87
Hamildoc **58**:73
Hampshire (HMS) **59**:131
Hampton Ferry (1934) **60**:210
Hamza I (1945) **57**:7
Hans Hemsoth (1894) **60**:239,241,249
Hans Krüger (1976) **60**:212,227
Hansa (1961) **58**:90
Happy Sunshine (1942) **58**:75
Harmattan (1930) **58**:118
Harraton (1930) **59**:147-8
Harry (1928) **57**:9
Haslemere (1925) **59**:138-9;**60**:200-3,206
Haslemere (HMS) **60**:206
Hawk (USS) **59**:157
Hazelbank (1977) **60**:214,216-7,219,227
Hazlehead (1959) **59**:178
He Feng (1979) **58**:104
He Ping 28 (1979) **58**:104
Headway (trawler) **59**:180
Heathdene (1898) **57**:28
Heather K. Wood (1960) (trawler) **59**:182
Heathside (1906) **60**:243
Heimfeld (1894) **60**:249
Helen Fairplay (1945) **57**:3,7
Helicina (1946) **59**:186
Helicon (1887) **59**:132
Hematite (1903) **57**:49
Heng Chang Lun (1973) **58**:105
Henriette (1943) **57**:14
Henriette Schulte (1977) **60**:220,227
Hercules (1910) **59**:142
Herm-S (1954) **57**:4
Heron (1937) **57**:38

Heyshott (1949) **59**:150
Hickory (lighter) **57**:10
Hill (1920) **58**:79
Hillglade (1921) **60**:248-9
Hillsider (1917) **57**:45
Hilsea (1930) **57**:38
Hoegh Clipper (1954) **57**:16
Hogland (1914) **60**:247
Holland XXIV **60**:235
Holmburn (1906) **60**:246
Holmside (1941) **59**:149
Holmwood (1912) **59**:133
Hopestar (1936) **57**:54
Hubro (1921) **58**:118
Hudson Deep (1953) **59**:151
Hun Jiang (1981) **58**:105
Huntsland **58**:84,94
Huntsville (1972) **58**:84,94
Hupeh **60**:226
Hyades (1899) **59**:133
Hyalina (1948) **59**:186
Hyang Ro Bong (1982) **58**:105
Hythe (1925) **59**:137,139;**60**:201-3,206-7
Hyundai Duke **58**:93

Iberia Star (1950) **58**:120-1
Icemaid (1936) **59**:148-9
Ilex (HMS) **57**:41
Ilse (1929) **59**:145
Imerina **57**:17
Imogen (HMS) **57**:41
Indian Endurance (1975) **60**:233
Indian Prince (anti-submarine trawler) **57**:45
Indium (1923) **57**:62
Indotrans Flores **60**:226
Induna (1891) **59**:130-1
Indus (tug) **57**:53
Indus (1951) **57**:15-6,18
Indus (1958) **58**:84
Ines Corrado **58**:118
Inflexible (HMS) **59**:133
Ingerfire (1905) **60**:244
Inston (1921) **60**:241,248
Inveritchen (1920) **60**:204
Invincible (HMS) **59**:133
Ioannis (1938) **58**:76
Ionian Reefer (1965) **58**:117
Iraouaddy (1953) **57**:19-20
Irene (1935) **60**:251
Irenes Hope (1953) **59**:151
Isis (HMS) **57**:41
Island Peak (1964) **58**:114
Isvania (1938) **58**:71
Ita (1908) **57**:58
Itajai Reefer (1964) **58**:113
Italia **58**:84
Ivan Topic (1920) **58**:72
Ivybank (1974) **60**:224,227

J. Milton (1872) **60**:194
Jacinth (1937) **57**:39
Jacques del Mar (1906) **60**:246
Jade II (1980) **58**:104
Jade III (1980) **58**:105
Jade Islands **58**:90
Jadotville (1956) **58**:120;**59**:161
Jaipur (1981) **58**:107
Janet Plym (1935) **60**:241,251
Jarrah (lighter) **57**:10
Java Maru (1902) **57**:26

261